ENTERTAINING ANGELS

DEDICATION

For two of my best friends – my wonderful daughter Rebecca,
and Gilli, her mother.
Without them this play would not have been written.

RE

Richard Everett

ENTERTAINING ANGELS

OBERON BOOKS
LONDON

WWW.OBERONBOOKS.COM

First published in 2009 by Oberon Books Ltd
521 Caledonian Road, London N7 9RH
Tel: +44 (0) 20 7607 3637 / Fax: +44 (0) 20 7607 3629
e-mail: info@oberonbooks.com
www.oberonbooks.com

PB ISBN: 9781840029673
E ISBN: 9781849435178

Cover photograph by Nobby Clark shows Penelope Keith as Grace
Copyright © Nobby Clark

Printed and bound by 4EDGE Limited, Hockley, Essex, UK.
eBook conversion by CPI Group (UK) Ltd, Croydon, CR0 4YY.

Visit www.oberonbooks.com to read more about all our books and
to buy them. You will also find features, author interviews and news
of any author events, and you can sign up for e-newsletters so that
you're always first to hear about our new releases.

Characters

GRACE,
aged sixty-one

RUTH,
her sister, aged early sixties

BARDOLPH,
Grace's husband, aged sixty something

JO,
Grace's daughter, aged early thirties

SARAH,
aged early thirties

SETTING
A vicarage garden

TIME
The present

This version of *Entertaining Angels* was first presented by Michael Codron and Theatre Royal Bath Productions at the Theatre Royal Bath on 21 September 2009, with the following cast:

GRACE, Penelope Keith

BARDOLPH, Benjamin Whitrow

RUTH, Polly Adams

JO, Carolyn Backhouse

SARAH, Claudia Elmhirst

Understudies: David Sparks, Debbi Blythe, Keeley Beresford

Director Alan Strachan

Designer Paul Farnsworth

Lighting Designer Jason Taylor

Sound Designer Ian Horrocks-Taylor

Composer Matthew Scott

A version of this play was previously presented at the Chichester Festival Theatre in May 2006.

Act One

A rural English vicarage garden.

The house to which it belongs is partly visible and accessible through garden doors. There is also a passageway down the side of the house that leads to an unseen front drive.

In the garden itself there is a garden bench, a small table and two small garden chairs. To one side of the garden is a greenhouse, but we only see the doorway and a small section of it. Between the greenhouse and the main house is an arbor or hedged archway leading to more of the garden and a stream somewhere beyond.

The bank of the stream (seen later) is a separate location set downstage/ wherever but which, for staging purposes, will merge with the garden. Beside the stream stands a tree and a small grassy mound.

GRACE appears from the house on the telephone. She is an ageless fifty/ sixty something who, in spite of her advancing years and brisk manner, has the endearing energy and poise of a younger woman.

GRACE: (*Phone.*) I'm going to take this in the garden Isabel...

She sits on the bench.

(*Phone.*) The vet... No, the vet I said. I had to take my sister Ruth to the vet... What?... No, no, no. We've acquired a hamster and it's got cystitis... Well, I don't know but apparently they do. Anyway, the hamster belongs to a neighbour who's gone on holiday so I had to take Ruth to the vet because she seems to be in charge of it. Ruth doesn't drive, she was accompanied by the hamster who, oddly enough, also doesn't drive, and all three of us – Ruth, me and Jeremiah – sallied forth at first light, leaving you with the answer machine... Jeremiah's the hamster, it's her nickname for it... From the Old Testament, I imagine, she's a missionary... No, my sister's the missionary not the hamster. Isabel, are you listening to anything I'm saying?

7

A voice from within the house comes into earshot...

SARAH: (*Off.*) This is the third time I've been here and the third time we've had this conversation.

GRACE reacts as SARAH appears from the house speaking on a mobile phone with an ear piece in...

(*Mobile phone.*) Well, I'm going outside to look.

SARAH, early thirties, a good looking woman in stylish everyday clothing. Irritated by the interruption, GRACE temporarily abandons her phone conversation.

(*Phone.*) No, I'm sorry but from here I definitely can, Nick. Even with the curtains drawn, if you started to undress now I could see the complete works.

SARAH wanders back into the house.

(*Phone.*) Far better to make that room the study and have the guest room upstairs.

As SARAH exits, GRACE resumes her phone conversation...

GRACE: (*Phone.*) Yes, I'm still here... Who is, who's more qualified?... Oh, the vet, yes. Well, they all are nowadays – more qualified than GPs... Well, quite, and there's no hanging about either. Show me a budgie that's had to wait nine months for a hip replacement... Oh blazes! Hold on a second can you, Isabel?... Ruth!... RUTH!

RUTH, of similar age to GRACE, whose plain and dishevelled appearance hides a natural beauty and warmth, crosses the stage in a gardening hat and pushing a noisy lawn mower.

Wretched woman... Ruth! Can't you see I'm on the...!

RUTH is oblivious and continues across the stage and vanishes.

(*Phone.*) No, it was my sister cutting the grass. You met her at the funeral... Who?... Oh yes! I did! Sweet girl. I saw her in Sainsbury's and she had it with her in a pram. Artificial insemination, I gather, we had quite a chat about it… Of course not, I was very tactful I said: 'congratulations. To look at it you'd never know.'

JO, a casually stylish and attractive woman, aged early thirties, saunters on looking at a pile of letters.

JO: I've sorted through most of these.

GRACE: (*Phone.*) Just a moment, Isabel.

JO: You really should have replied to them, you know.

GRACE: (*To JO.*) Are you talking to me?

JO: The urgent ones, anyway. There's really no excuse.

GRACE: Excuse for what?

JO: An afternoon that's all it would take.

GRACE: I thought you were going home.

JO: I am. Shortly. I'm trying to make myself useful.

GRACE: The most useful thing you could do is put those back where you found them.

JO: You've been saying that for weeks.

GRACE: And I'll probably keep on saying it, now put them back.

JO: They're from your friends.

GRACE: Your father's friends. Parishioners mostly, and half of them couldn't even spell his name correctly. Look, I'm trying to have a phone conversation and… Oh dear God… Ruth!

RUTH returns noisily with the mower…

Can't you do that somewhere else?!… Ruth!

RUTH: Sorry?!

GRACE: Could you please do that somewhere else?! I'm on the… (*Phone.*) I'm sorry about this Isabel.

9

RUTH: (*Unhooking grass bucket.*)… What do you think of my diagonals? I prefer diagonals. They look rather good, I think.

As RUTH ambles off to empty the grass bucket, leaving the mower idling, SARAH wanders out of the house again still talking on the mobile phone…

SARAH: (*Phone.*) And then, if we have, what – more than eight, say? – we can spill out here into the garden?

GRACE: I say! Excuse me!

SARAH: (*Phone.*) Well, if it's raining they won't spill out here, will they? They'll spill out somewhere else.

GRACE: Excuse…!

SARAH: (*Phone.*) Well yes, the downstairs toilet if necessary. Why do you have to find fault with everything?

GRACE: Excuse me!

SARAH pulls the ear piece from her ears.

SARAH: I'm so sorry, Mrs Thomas. Am I disturbing you?

GRACE: Yes. You are. This is still my house and I do still happen to live here.

As the mower continues to idle noisily, RUTH returns with the now-empty grass bucket…

RUTH: It's remarkably satisfying doing stripes. In Uganda, grass is a sign of wealth and…

GRACE strides angrily across to the mower and releases the clutch lever. The mower sets off on its own. RUTH hurries after it and exits.

SARAH: I'm almost done, Mrs Thomas, then I can leave you in peace.

As SARAH exits into the house…

(*Phone.*) I have to go, Nicholas – I'm disturbing Mrs Thomas.

JO remains. GRACE puts the phone to her ear again.

GRACE: (*Phone.*) Isabel, this is hopeless. I'll have to call you back.

GRACE hangs up. JO looks at her. After a few seconds…

JO: You really are the most extraordinarily difficult woman, you know.

GRACE: I try, certainly.

An elderly man appears in a waistcoat, shirt sleeves and panama hat. As he ambles across the stage, GRACE turns and watches him. He walks between JO and GRACE and then disappears into the greenhouse. JO doesn't acknowledge him at all but she watches GRACE watching the man. After a few seconds…

JO: Who was that?

GRACE: Who was who?

JO: On the phone.

GRACE: Oh. Isabel Greene. She means well but honestly I do find this whole business awfully tiresome.

JO: What business?

GRACE: Being a widow.

JO: So you'll do these letters, will you?

GRACE: It's open season for everyone's sympathy.

JO: Mum?

GRACE: The worst thing is becoming the vanguard of other people's faith. 'The vicar's croaked it. Let's see how she fares, let's see if this stuff stands up at all.' I was expected to smile, you know.

JO: When?

GRACE: At the funeral.

JO: By who?

GRACE: Assorted lunatics. Intended as encouragement, of course. The only thing to make me smile that day was Joyce Bannerman's face.

JO: Yes I heard about that.

GRACE: Stupid woman. She came up to me after the service and said what a wonderful occasion it had been.

JO: I know.

GRACE: 'Has it, my dear?' I said. 'I'm so glad. We should do it more often.' Her face was a picture. 'Your husband's looking a bit peaky,' I said, 'any chance of him popping his clogs and you having a crack at it?'

JO: She was very upset.

GRACE: I should hope she was. I've never seen that fixed and heavenly smile dislodged before. I sometimes wonder, you know, about what would happen to these people if they actually made contact with the real world.

JO: What people?

GRACE: The ones I've spent forty years pouring tea for. I worked it out the other day. Since your father and I began parish life, I've boiled seven thousand gallons of water and poured two hundred thousand cups of tea.

JO: You've loved every minute of it.

GRACE turns to JO and fixes her with a stare.

GRACE: I've also baked four thousand six hundred medium-sized guiches and personally made two tons of short crust pastry. And for what? So that I can smile as expected at my husband's funeral and have asinine remarks made to me at the west door?

JO: You didn't do it for them. You did it for Dad.

GRACE: Yes. Didn't I, just.

JO: Which is why, for his sake at least, you should reply to these letters.

RUTH re-enters out of breath and mopping her brow…

RUTH: Sorry about that. I don't have one of those in Uganda.

GRACE: One of what?

RUTH: What?

GRACE: Ruth dear, I don't know if it's because you're a missionary but you have a remarkable gift for conversations that no one can follow.

RUTH: Sorry.

GRACE: And stop apologising too. You're becoming a habitual penitent – which is presumably why you became a missionary in the first place.

RUTH: I'm a 'mission partner', Grace. I work full time for a church relief agency.

GRACE: What don't you have one of in Uganda?

RUTH: What?… Oh! A phone. Like yours. Telephones in general we have obviously, but I don't have one without wires and things.

GRACE: Really. Fascinating. Your aunt only has a phone with wires, Jo. Did you know that?

JO: Why don't you go out or something?

GRACE: I don't want to go out. Why would I want to go out?

JO: Because it isn't fair.

GRACE: On whom?

JO: On anyone… (*Pointing toward the house.*) … But especially her. She's got to look round, it's going to be her home.

GRACE: At the moment it's still my home.

JO: A couple of weeks ago you couldn't wait to see the back of the place.

GRACE: I can't.

JO: You were even talking about going to a 'bed and breakfast'.

GRACE doesn't respond.

RUTH: Grace dear, why don't you go and visit someone – as you did when they came before?

GRACE: I don't want to visit anyone. I've spent my life visiting people.

SARAH re-appears from the house, trying to be unobtrusive.

JO: (*To GRACE, whispered.*) You could at least speak to her. She's very nice and it's their first parish, you might actually be able to help her if you set your mind to it.

SARAH: I'm just off now, Mrs Thomas.

JO looks at GRACE who looks back at JO and then GRACE switches on a huge smile to SARAH and bursts into 'warm and sympathetic' mode as we see the welcoming clergy wife in all her glory.

GRACE: No, don't! Come and sit down, come and tell me all about yourself! Jo, get some tea organised. Ruth go and mow or something. Sit down, my dear. Do sit down. Right here next to me.

RUTH exits. JO suppresses a laugh. SARAH pulls up a chair.

SARAH: Well, I don't want to intrude.

GRACE: No, no. Perish the thought.

SARAH: I must say, it would be nice to chat.

GRACE: Of course… Jo darling. Could you manage that?

JO: Yes. Of course.

JO exits.

GRACE: I'm sorry I wasn't here on your other visit.

SARAH: I quite understood. It can't be easy and your daughter has been terribly helpful.

GRACE: Has she? Oh good. She's a psychotherapist, you know.

SARAH: No, I didn't know that.

GRACE: Professionally trained to be helpful.

SARAH: Well, she showed me the church and walked me round the village and told me all about your life here over coffee in the tea shop. I have to tell you Mrs Thomas, I am quite excited.

GRACE: Are you? I'm so glad... What about?

SARAH: Taking over the parish. We both are. We work very well together, Nicholas and I.

GRACE: Do you.

SARAH: He's a very creative man.

GRACE: Is he. Remarkable. Who's Nicholas?

SARAH: My husband?

GRACE: Ah, yes.

SARAH: Everyone tells me how lucky I am.

GRACE: Well. What do we know – we're just the wives. Soon to be canonised, no doubt.

SARAH: Who is?

GRACE: Your husband. Ha!... Don't fret, my dear, I'm joking. Although, they'll certainly treat him as such when he gets here. Fell at my husband's feet they did – especially the women.

SARAH: Did they? Aah!

GRACE: I think, for some, the arrival of a new vicar is a bit like having a new boyfriend. Anyway, you've nothing to fear from this lot – a few nips and tucks and the occasional outbreak of botox – but exceedingly unattractive, most of them. So, full of plans, I expect?

SARAH: Oh yes. Brim full.

GRACE: Well, here's one worth avoiding: spiritual revival. The last thing anyone needs is reviving, I assure you – and it plays havoc with your sex life. Bardy went through a brief spell of it and I almost left him – services that wouldn't finish and the most frightful outbreak of men's prayer breakfasts. Ghastly things. I told Bardy, 'If you insist on having over-lunched businessmen engaged in religious fervour at six in the morning, you can take them into the greenhouse. I find starting the day difficult enough without a circus in my kitchen.'

SARAH smiles at GRACE uncertainly.

I'm not being over-bearing, am I? People say I'm becoming over-bearing.

SARAH: No. Not at all.

GRACE: I say 'people' – my family mostly. They think I've gone potty. Do you have children?

SARAH: No.

GRACE: Still in the planning?

SARAH: Yes… Well… You know…

GRACE: Don't leave it too late. Have lots of them too – there's nothing like a big family for keeping you on your toes and God in his place.

SARAH: Well. When there's time. We'll be rushed off our feet to begin with – I will, anyway. Nicholas will be the one with time on his hands.

GRACE: Ha! A woman after my own heart. Vicars are the only profession I know where the very thing they're being paid to do is the very thing they expect everyone else to do for them.

SARAH: I don't think you quite understand.

GRACE: I've seen it all from very close quarters, my dear. Work-shy, every man jack of them.

SARAH: I'm the new priest-in-charge here, Mrs Thomas – not my husband, at least for the *inter regnum.*

GRACE looks at SARAH, expressionless.

Nicholas runs a frozen food company. Fish, mostly. Pacific prawns, crab, scampi. He's developed a special process for dry-freezing and thinking of going into trout.

JO re-enters.

JO: The kettle's on.

GRACE: Oh, good. With the kettle on and God in his heaven, we've not a care in the world – have we, Sarah?

GRACE gets up and wanders distractedly over to the greenhouse and peers in.

SARAH: I've just been singing your praises to your mother. You never told me you were a psychotherapist!

JO: You never asked.

SARAH: Didn't I? All that time we spent chatting – how very un-pastoral of me.

JO: Actually, I thought you might see me as the opposition.

SARAH: No! Good heavens. I think what we do is rather similar. We both hear confession, we just do it in different outfits.

JO sees GRACE returning from the greenhouse.

JO: Look, I'm sorry about… (*Pointing to GRACE.*)

SARAH: Oh nonsense, it's a difficult time. And being a woman curate prepares you for most things.

JO: Yes, I can imagine.

SARAH: One old boy kneeling at the altar said: 'sorry love. I'm not taking communion from someone who doesn't shave every morning.'

JO: You're joking. What did you say?

SARAH: I leaned down and whispered that I'd had my legs waxed the day before and did that count?

They laugh.

He was so shocked his mouth fell open so I shoved in the wafer.

They laugh more, then JO notices GRACE returning to the bench.

JO: I'm sure you'll be very happy here. Mum and Dad were… weren't you Mum?

GRACE: I'm still here, in case you hadn't noticed.

SARAH: Things have to move forward, Mrs Thomas.

GRACE: Do they?

SARAH: Yes.

GRACE: Forward.

SARAH: Yes.

GRACE: Why?

SARAH: (*Taking GRACE's hand.*) … Your husband's gone now, Mrs Thomas.

GRACE leans forward to SARAH.

GRACE: You're a very observant woman, Sarah... So.
A female vicar. Does this put us on the cutting-edge, d'you
suppose?

JO: Mum.

GRACE: My husband's gone so I'm to be evicted – is that what
you're all saying?

SARAH: Not at all.

GRACE: What, then?

SARAH: Your husband has moved on and he would want you
to do the same, don't you think?

GRACE: I love this, don't you? How old are you, Sarah?

SARAH: Thirty-one.

GRACE: Thirty-one. I'm sixty-one. What can you possibly
have to say to me about life, death or anything else, that I
couldn't possibly have thought for myself?

JO: Oh, God.

GRACE: I'm talking to the vicar. If you want to pray, the shop's
open. (*To SARAH.*) We always kept it open, I hope you'll do
the same.

JO: Sarah is just trying to help, Mum.

GRACE: I don't need help.

SARAH: It's fine, Jo, really... (*To GRACE.*) Mrs Thomas, from all
that I hear your husband was a remarkable man. He served
God and the people of this parish faithfully for many years.
No one is evicting anyone, but this house was part of his
work, and now it passes on to his successor.

GRACE: *My* work isn't done so why should I go?

SARAH: Mrs Thomas, I'm a little confused. I understood
from the bishop that you wanted to leave here as soon as
possible.

GRACE: Oh I do. I most certainly do… Oh look! It's gardening Gertie!

RUTH enters mopping her brow and collapses in a chair.

RUTH: I'm absolutely parched.

GRACE: Good. Well, the kettle's boiled, so you can make some tea. Chop! Chop!

JO: It's all right, I'll do it.

GRACE: No, no. Let Ruth do it – it'll stop her running round my garden like a demented gnome.

SARAH: Actually Jo, Nick asked me to have a look at your stream. (*To GRACE.*) As I said, he's thinking of going into trout.

GRACE: Is he.

SARAH: Yes.

GRACE: Trout.

SARAH: Yes. (*To JO.*) He said on our last visit that you mentioned a dam to him?

JO: Yes. Did I not show it to you? Follow me.

JO leads off. SARAH is about to follow but turns to GRACE.

SARAH: Mrs Thomas?… (*Taking GRACE's hand.*) … I'm so glad we've managed to chat at last.

GRACE: Oh so am I.

SARAH goes. Pause. GRACE wanders towards the greenhouse. RUTH gets up…

RUTH: She seems nice enough.

GRACE: Oh, very… 'nice'.

RUTH: So. How rude have you been?

GRACE: I haven't been rude at all.

RUTH: That rude. Dear me. You were difficult as a child, you've been difficult ever since. God knows what you'll be like when you're old.

GRACE: I am old.

RUTH: Nonsense. You're a few years younger than me.

GRACE: I'm old and you're extremely old. Go and make the tea.

RUTH: I thought I might water the toms first.

GRACE turns on her suddenly.

GRACE: You stay out of that greenhouse.

RUTH: They'll die, Grace.

GRACE: Let them!

GRACE picks up a fork from the barrow, threatens RUTH with it whilst blocking the greenhouse door.

RUTH: Very well. I'll make the tea, then.

GRACE: Yes, you do that.

RUTH grabs the fork off GRACE, throws it in the wheelbarrow and sets off toward the house.

RUTH: (*Going.*) Difficult and potty with it.

Brief pause, then GRACE starts talking to someone…

GRACE: A female vicar. What do you make of that?

The elderly man re-appears from the greenhouse. It is BARDOLPH, GRACE's husband, a willowy man with a slight stoop and a large warm face. He has a watering can in his hand.

BARDY: Saw it coming years ago.

GRACE: You never predicted a frock in the pulpit.

BARDY: I predicted a woman in Downing Street.

GRACE: That was different. And anyway she wasn't a woman, she was a dictator with bosoms.

BARDY wanders back into the greenhouse. GRACE leans on the doorway and talks to him inside as he potters about, disappearing and reappearing, watering, potting seeds, etc. And occasionally bringing stuff out.

I suppose the next thing will be a lady bishop.

BARDY: Oh, I think that's going a little far.

GRACE: Ha! That will divide the sheep from the old goats.

BARDY looks at his pots.

BARDY: None of these little plants could have grown, Grace, if they had not first been divided.

GRACE: Yes, I know. Division and the church are ancient bed-fellows.

BARDY: As far back as the first century. The Council at Jerusalem.

GRACE: And you know what they were rowing about then?

BARDY: Circumcision.

GRACE: Foreskins, Bardy. They were arguing about whether a believer could still be accepted if someone hadn't first chopped off the end of his willy.

BARDY: Circumcision was a sacred Hebrew rite dating back to Abraham.

GRACE: When God looks one way, the church always seems to be looking the other.

BARDY: The point is they sorted it out and the church grew.

GRACE: Just as well – otherwise when people today line up for communion, the sidesmen would have to do a security check and peer down the front of men's trousers.

Pause. GRACE watches BARDY as he potters on.

What am I going to do, Bardy?

BARDY: The vicar's right. You'll have to go, old thing.

GRACE: I'm not ready to go.

BARDY: Neither was I, but there it is. The clock ticks and everything moves on.

GRACE: That's easy for you to say. That's easy enough for you to say from where you are. What's it like, by the way?

BARDY: Oh… You know.

GRACE: No, I don't know. Tell me.

BARDY: So-so.

GRACE: So-so? It's got to be better than so-so.

BARDY: Hard to describe, really. Not how I imagined at all.

GRACE: Wonderful. You've spent forty years telling everyone it's eternal bliss, and you get there and say it's so-so.

BARDY: Well, I'm still a bit of a new boy.

GRACE: We'd better amend the gospel reading for sunday. 'In my father's house are many mansions most of which are so-so.'

GRACE starts pacing the garden restlessly.

I think I'm going to be difficult about this, Bardy. I'm going to be extremely difficult about the whole thing.

BARDY: You've always been difficult about everything.

GRACE: Everyone's been saying that to me today.

BARDY: You do keep changing your mind, Grace.

GRACE: I'll leave when I'm ready. Why should I go if I don't feel like it?

BARDY appears at the doorway with earthy hands and a trowel.

BARDY: Because I'm dead!... And it's how the system works. You should try and keep busy, take your mind of things.

GRACE: I don't want my mind taken off anything. My mind's fine where it is.

BARDY: No point in being maudlin.

GRACE: I'm not being maudlin.

BARDY: Standing here talking to me's pretty maudlin.

GRACE: Would you rather I didn't?

BARDY: You need to be distracted. Try spending more time with our daughter.

GRACE: She's depressing.

BARDY: She's in pain.

GRACE: I'm in pain.

BARDY: Then you've something in common for once.

GRACE: At least I'm interesting. At least my pain keeps everyone amused and alert, she's just dreary.

BARDY: It was a dreary thing for him to have done.

GRACE: Trust Jo to marry a man with his brains in his underpants.

BARDY: He wasn't known as the parish organist for nothing.

BARDY disappears into the greenhouse. GRACE sits on the bench. The sudden sound of rushing water. Light change to...

JO and SARAH appear by the stream...

JO: Careful. It's slippery.

SARAH: It's beautiful.

JO: I used to play here for hours when I was a child.

JO stands and takes in the vista.

The sound of water, there's nothing like it. My father loved it down here. He used to write all his sermons sitting under this tree.

SARAH: I'm not surprised. It's an inspiring place.

JO: He died down there in the stream.

SARAH: Really? Where?

JO: Just there, on the edge.

JO sits on the grass and closes her eyes. SARAH peers over the bank.

SARAH: What happened?

JO: Not sure. My mother found him in the weeds. Heart failure, the doctor said.

Pause. SARAH crouches down to the stream and dips her hand in the water. She scoops some up and lets it trickle through her fingers, then cups her hand and splashes her face. JO opens her eyes and watches this.

Practising for your first baptism?

SARAH smiles.

SARAH: Rather a nice idea actually. I could bring families down here to gather on the bank.

JO: You'll have to be careful, it gets quite murky in the middle.

SARAH: (*Suddenly recoiling.*) ... Ooh! What was that?! I saw something move.

JO: A water rat, probably, they live in the bank. Dad and I used to give them names and made up stories about them.

SARAH tentatively peers into the stream.

SARAH: There!... I just saw its head.

JO: Tell me something, Sarah. Why did you become a priest?

SARAH: Why?

JO: Yes. Why?

SARAH: The usual reasons.

JO: Which are?

SARAH: Same as you, probably. Why did you become a psychotherapist?

JO: It pays the bills, the hours are civilised, and I like spending time with nutters.

SARAH: Well. There you go.

JO: Very good. So, what made you do it? Were you always religious?

SARAH: God, no… I can't see a dam here anywhere.

JO: Most of it's washed away but the remains are over there. So, come on what happened?

SARAH: It's a long story. I'm not sure this is the time.

JO: I told you, I like stories.

SARAH: Well…just after we were married I went through a difficult time. I was very confused, I didn't know who I was or what I wanted – I wasn't even sure if I was with the right man. All in all I ended up in a bit of a heap.

JO: So you turned to God?

SARAH: Hardly, no. I turned to the French polisher… How long since it worked?

JO: Excuse me?

SARAH: The dam.

JO: The French polisher?!

SARAH: He spent two days bending over my grannie's table trying to restore it.

JO: You had an affair?

SARAH: Hamish. Terribly young. I can't think what possessed me.

JO: His very cute bum, by the sound of it. Oh…my…God!

SARAH: With all due respect Jo, I don't think 'Oh my God!' is the right response for a therapist, is it?

JO: I'm off duty and I'm not your therapist. How on earth did Hamish the French polisher get you to 'dearly beloved' status?

SARAH: Through a lot of angst and a remarkable husband.

JO: He found out?

SARAH: I told him. He was extraordinary. He's been an absolute rock to me ever since.

JO: A rock. I was married to one of those.

SARAH: How long has it been?

JO: Almost two years. My married friends keep trying to set me up with their weird relatives and my single friends keep trying to set me up with their weird cast-offs. I feel like a house with multiple agents that no one can shift. You don't by any chance have Hamish's number do you?

SARAH: No. I don't.

JO: Pity. Anyway, you still haven't explained the big leap.

SARAH: It wasn't a leap so much as…well… I came face to face with something scary and dangerous.

JO: The affair.

SARAH: No, forgiveness… (*Peering over the bank.*) … It wouldn't take much to put it back together, would it?

JO: Just like that? He forgave you?

SARAH: No. Not just like that. But he did.

JO looks at her, unsure of how to react. SARAH becomes aware of this.

I know. I asked him if he could stop being super-human and start throwing things and walk out. He said he would like to but the trouble was he loved me, so…

JO: Did you love him?

SARAH: Until that point, I hadn't been sure. Then I knew that I did. It was a moment for me, the start…of all kinds of things.

JO: And your route to God.

SARAH: Sort of… (*Peering into the stream.*) … A weekend's work? What do you think?

JO: I think, as a matter of Christian duty, you should give Hamish's number to everyone you meet.

SARAH: Yes. Well. I'll pray about it certainly. Perhaps we should be getting back… (*Peering back to the stream.*) … Nicholas will enjoy restoring that.

JO: You've surprised me, Sarah.

SARAH: Have I?

JO: Yes.

SARAH: Oh dear.

JO: I really hope you'll be happy here.

SARAH: I hope I'm up to the task – I'm not at all sure I'm ready.

JO: Oh, I think you'll be a breath of fresh air.

JO starts to lead off.

SARAH: Jo, what I've just told you, I don't think it's appropriate information for your mother, do you?

JO: Why? She'll love it. She'll probably use it in her farewell article in the parish mag.

SARAH: No, seriously – I don't think…

JO: Sarah, trust me – I'm a therapist.

JO smiles. SARAH laughs. They leave.

Back in the garden, GRACE still sits on the bench.

GRACE: Were you ever unfaithful, Bardy?

BARDY reappears the greenhouse door.

BARDY: To whom?

GRACE: To me. Who d'you think?… Bardy?

BARDY: Yes?

GRACE: You're hesitating.

BARDY: I'm thinking.

GRACE: What about? You're not counting, are you?

BARDY: I'm pondering the word 'faithful'.

GRACE: Pondering!? You've passed on, Bardolph, the truth should spring from your lips with speed and alacrity.

BARDY: Passing on doesn't make you perfect, you know.

GRACE: I thought that was the whole point. You're not telling me the Buddhists are right, are you? We haven't all got to flog our way to perfection by becoming giraffes and fleas.

BARDY: You don't just leave and switch the light out, that's all I'm saying. It's a journey.

GRACE: Bardy?

BARDY: Yes?

GRACE: You're not in purgatory, are you?

BARDY: No, no. I did all that in the parish.

RUTH re-appears from the house with a tea tray.

RUTH: Overgrown. The whole place is overgrown.

GRACE: I beg your pardon?

RUTH: The weeds. I was looking out of the kitchen window –
they're completely taking over.

GRACE: They're in good company then.

RUTH: Sorry?

GRACE: Nothing.

RUTH plonks the tea tray down on the table.

RUTH: Where is everyone?

GRACE: Jo's taken the fish wife to look at the stream –
something to do with trout, I believe.

RUTH: Golly it's warm. It's like being back home... Except for
the smell of cut grass.

*RUTH shuts here eyes and fans her face with her hat. GRACE
eyes her.*

Mmmh...freshly mown grass. It smells...of England.

GRACE: Ruth dear, there's something I've been meaning to
ask you.

RUTH: What's that?

GRACE: What are you doing here?

RUTH: What do you mean?

GRACE: I mean, apart from smelling England, what are you
doing here?

RUTH: I'm staying with you.

GRACE: I'm acutely aware of that, but when are you going?

RUTH: Back to Uganda, you mean?

GRACE: Yes.

RUTH: I don't know. I have an open ticket. Am I in the way or something?

GRACE: Yes.

RUTH: Oh.

GRACE: I just don't know what you're doing here, that's all.

RUTH: I want to be with you, of course.

GRACE: No, you don't. You want to be handing out bibles and antibiotics to those poor defenceless creatures in Uganda.

RUTH: Grace, you're my sister.

GRACE: I know that, but we're not close. It's not as though we're close.

RUTH: We are.

GRACE: We're not. We've never been close.

RUTH: We've often been close.

GRACE: When?

RUTH: When we were children.

GRACE: But we're not children. We're old and we're distant.

RUTH: Look, is it going anywhere this conversation or are you just being difficult again?

GRACE: What is this obsession that everyone has with my being difficult? All I want is a simple answer to a simple question: I want to know when you're going home!

SARAH and JO return from the stream.

RUTH: Ah, here they are. I've done mugs not cups and saucers. I hope that's all right.

GRACE: (*To SARAH.*) You'll have to forgive her – she's a missionary. Were you ever a missionary, Sarah?

SARAH: No, but I worked for Christian Aid when I was a student.

GRACE: Splendid. What marvellous people we all are. How was the stream?

SARAH: Fine, yes. Nicholas will love it.

GRACE: Oh good. Do you think you can breed in it?

SARAH: I'm sorry?

GRACE: Trout.

SARAH: Oh!… Yes. A bit of mending and fixing but he'll make something of it, I'm sure.

BARDY re-appears at the greenhouse door. GRACE gets up and walks over to him.

JO: Mum? Where are you going?

GRACE: Carry on. I'll be back in a minute.

The three women gather round the tea table while GRACE talks to BARDY by the greenhouse.

GRACE: Bardy, I want to ask you something.

BARDY: I'm listening.

GRACE: Where you are, can you… I mean, do they let you do your Tommy Cooper impressions?

BARDY: Oh yes. And I think they're getting better. Shame you can't see them.

GRACE: I wish I could. I do miss your bedtime routine. Do one for me now, just this once.

BARDY turns his panama round and ruffles the sides of his hair and does a not very good impression of Tommy Cooper.

BARDY: 'Two cannibals cooking a clown. One says to the other "Does this taste funny to you?"' Ha! ha! ha!

GRACE claps her hands and laughs.

GRACE: I love it. It's terrible. Even in heaven it hasn't improved.

BARDY: It helps if I'm in pyjamas.

The others turn and look at her but GRACE ignores them. Her mood changes suddenly.

GRACE: Are you angry with me, Bardy?

BARDY: Angry?

GRACE: You know very well what I mean.

BARDY: You did what you did, old thing.

GRACE: But was it wrong?

BARDY: Does it matter?

GRACE: To me. Yes.

BARDY: Why?

GRACE: Because... I have to live with it.

BARDY: And if I tell you it wasn't, will that make it easier?

GRACE: I'd just like to know...if I'm forgiven.

At the tea gathering, RUTH notices GRACE.

RUTH: Jo, she's doing it again.

JO: I've spoken to the doctor, we both think it'll pass... (*To SARAH.*) ... We keep finding her talking to herself.

SARAH: It's not uncommon. She probably thinks she's talking to your father. Does she get distressed at all?

RUTH: No. Just difficult.

SARAH: Then I'm sure the doctor's right. Leave her be, and given time she'll settle down.

GRACE notices JO and SARAH looking at her...

GRACE: They're doing it again, Bardy. They're talking about me.

She smiles and waves at them. They all smile and wave back.

JO: Your tea's here.

GRACE: In a minute… (*To BARDY.*) They think I've gone potty, you know.

BARDY: Yes.

GRACE: It's rather amusing. I can do and say exactly as I please.

BARDY: No change there, then.

GRACE: Oh Bardolph! I've spent my whole life accommodating you. How can you say such a thing?

BARDY pauses, take his hat off and mops his brow with a hanky.

BARDY: You know, Grace, it's not me that's angry, is it? It's the other way round.

GRACE: What do you mean?

BARDY: All those years of unspoken resentment just had to come out, didn't they?

Pause. GRACE ponders.

GRACE: I did it for you, Bardy.

BARDY: Not for yourself, Grace?

GRACE: I loved you.

BARDY: I loved you too.

GRACE: Don't do this to me. It isn't fair. You see things from where you are, don't you. You see it all.

BARDY: Go and have tea.

BARDY disappears into the greenhouse and shuts the door.

GRACE: Bardy, don't go… Please!

The others watch her.

RUTH: Grace, dear – you asked me to make tea, and now it's just sitting here getting cold!

GRACE turns and looks at them all looking back at her…

GRACE: What?

RUTH: Your tea.

GRACE: Bugger my tea.

GRACE sets off through the arch in the hedge.

JO: Where are you going?

GRACE: For a walk! I'm going for a walk! And when I come back I would like all of you, without exception, to have left my house!

GRACE goes.

JO: I'll go after her.

RUTH: No, it's all right, I'll go. You stay here.

RUTH exits in the direction that GRACE went.

SARAH: I'd better get going. Shall I help you clear this?

JO: No, leave it. I'm sorry about all that.

SARAH: Oh, it couldn't matter less.

JO: Why don't you and Nicholas come over to my place for a meal sometime?

SARAH: Um… Yes.

JO: No?

SARAH: Yes. Of course. Look Jo, I'm feeling slightly uncomfortable.

JO: Well, I'm not surprised. She's so volatile at the moment.

SARAH: No. I meant about our conversation… Earlier.

JO: Oh for heaven's sake, Sarah – you don't think I'm shocked do you?

SARAH: No.

JO: Good.

SARAH: It's just that… Well… It's not the whole story by a long chalk and I don't know how happy Nick would be.

JO: If I knew?

SARAH: Yes.

JO: Well, I'm hardly going to blurt it out over a casserole, am I? 'So Nicholas, I hear your wife once shagged a French polisher.'

SARAH: No, obviously – obviously not.

JO: I do do it for a living, you know – not shagging French polishers – I mean confidentiality.

SARAH: Yes, I realise that. I rather wish I hadn't said anything, that's all.

JO starts loading the tea tray.

JO: Doesn't it sort of go with the job? 'Tell us how you saw the light, vicar?' Don't you get asked that quite often?

SARAH: Yes.

JO: Well, you'd better get your story straight, Sarah. You can't kick off your coffee mornings with: 'My road to enlightenment all began with Hamish's arse'. Well, you could actually – you'd have them enthralled.

JO laughs. SARAH doesn't.

I'm sorry, I'm being flippant.

Brief pause.

SARAH: It wasn't just the affair, Jo.

JO: What wasn't?

SARAH hesitates, she looks troubled. She looks at JO. Then…

SARAH: I have to go.

SARAH reaches for her bag and starts fumbling for keys.

JO: Sarah?

SARAH: I'm not really ready for this job – in fact, to be brutally honest, I probably shouldn't be doing the job at all.

JO: What?

SARAH: Where are my blasted keys?… You've been very kind Jo but I'd appreciate it if you kept this conversation to yourself.

JO: Sarah… Hold on…

SARAH: No, the traffic and so on… Where the blazes have I put them?

JO: Perhaps you should talk to your bishop or something?

SARAH: Probably yes.

JO: I know he's a bloke and will probably say it's the time of the month.

SARAH: Thank you, yes. I'll bear it in mind… Wretched things. I had them earlier. Maybe I left them in the hall.

SARAH hurries into the house. JO follows.

JO: Look, why don't you pop down on Sunday? I'll be here all day – no need to phone – and we can chat properly… Sarah?

SARAH comes out again before JO can follow her in.

SARAH: I might. I'll see… (*Finding keys.*) Here they are. Right… Well… I'll see myself out. Bye Jo, and thank you again – and thank your mother for me, will you?

SARAH hurries off.

JO: Yes, of course… Bye… Sarah.

SARAH has gone. JO looks bemused for a moment and then picks up the tea tray and exits into the house.

The sound of rushing water again as the lights cross fade to the stream. GRACE re-enters. She walks carefully as she makes her way along the bank.

GRACE: Bardy? Are you down here?

BARDY wanders on with a notepad and pen…

BARDY: Over here, old thing. I'm just finishing my sermon for Sunday. Want to hear it?

GRACE: Not particularly.

BARDY: It's about Christ and the fig tree.

GRACE: Jo's just phoned. She's coming to lunch.

BARDY: It's that odd passage when he curses the fig tree.

GRACE: On her own by the sounds of it so I don't think things are any better.

BARDY: Know the one I mean?

GRACE: Mmmh? Yes, vaguely. He was hungry or something so he hurled abuse at it for not having any fruit – like me in Sainsbury's when they've run out of bread, the only difference being I send for the manager. The stream looks very green and murky today, I wish you wouldn't sit so near it.

BARDY: The stream and I are old friends.

GRACE: Well, don't get carried away and try walking on it. Bardy I want to talk to you.

BARDY: In a moment. Hear me out, I want your opinion. The line I've taken is that he was re-establishing his authority over the created order.

GRACE sighs and looks long-suffering.

GRACE: By cursing a fig tree.

BARDY: Yes.

GRACE: Well, it was a start I suppose.

BARDY: The point I'm making is that what is commonly regarded as an obscure incident that has had theologians scratching their heads for decades, is really quite simple – as simple, in fact, as it is profound: Christ the son of the maker-of-all-things steps into a dysfunctional world to re-establish his dominion over it… What do you think?

Pause.

GRACE: That's it is it?

BARDY: No good?

GRACE: And he was to do this by yelling obscenities at a fig tree.

BARDY: Not obscenities, no.

GRACE: How do you know? You weren't there. I should think the air was midnight blue. And anyway, if my memory serves me correctly, the tree wasn't even in season.

BARDY: No, true.

GRACE: So to expect it to have fruit, was rather unreasonable. Nothing short of a holy tantrum, in fact.

BARDY: Grace, you're missing the point.

GRACE: Am I? Sorry. I was just wondering how Christ cursing a fig tree will help a single mother in a high-rise get to Tesco's when her husband hasn't paid her maintenance and the lift is broken and full of urine?

BARDY: What?

GRACE: Or save the drowning children in Mozambique from a certain, miserable and untimely death?

BARDY: Fine. You don't like it.

GRACE: It doesn't matter whether I like it, Bardy. It doesn't matter whether anyone likes it. What matters is whether it's true, and we can't know that because we weren't there. He was angry. That's all we know so preach about that if you must – or better still, don't preach at all.

BARDY: Are you all right, old thing? You sound a little off colour.

GRACE: The world is full of words, Bardy, we're drowning in the bloody things!

BARDY: So we hold fast to the word of God.

GRACE: I could find you ten Anglican vicars who would say that and none of them agree on what 'the word of God' meant. The Bible is full of things we would rather not know and decidedly lacking in the things we would.

BARDY: Such as?

GRACE: What did he look like?

BARDY: Who?… Oh, well, that's quite deliberate. 'He hath no comeliness that we should look at him.'

GRACE: So was he fat, do you think?

BARDY: Fat?

GRACE: Yes. Was Jesus fat? What d'you think?

BARDY: Of course he wasn't fat. What a frightful thing to say.

GRACE: How do you know? He was a middle-aged, middle-class, middle-eastern rabbi who ate well and dined with the rich. I'd say his diet would have certainly have made him portly, possibly even rotund. That would have given Holman Hunt a problem, painting 'The Light of the World' with a fat Messiah.

BARDY: Grace dearest, I have a sermon to preach on Sunday – what has any of this to do with Christ and the fig tree?

Brief pause as GRACE looks at him wearily.

GRACE: Nothing, Bardy. Nothing at all. I came to tell you that Jo, your daughter, is coming to lunch and I think her marriage is on the rocks. I'm very worried so do you think you could talk to her?

RUTH approaches…

RUTH: (*Off.*) Grace?!

GRACE: Oh God!

GRACE is barely able to contain her frustration. As BARDY wanders off, RUTH approaches…

RUTH: There you are. What are you doing?

Pause as GRACE watches BARDY go.

GRACE: Remembering. What are you doing?

RUTH: Coming to find you.

GRACE: Well, you've managed that so now you can go.

RUTH: Bardy loved it down here, didn't he?

GRACE: Do you need me for something?

RUTH: Jo was telling me, he used to prepare all his sermons under that tree.

GRACE: Indeed he did. He also hated being disturbed so I used to leave him alone. I don't like being disturbed either so perhaps you could do the same?

RUTH: How long is this going to go on, Grace?

GRACE turns and looks at her.

GRACE: Ruth, I've hardly seen you for thirty years, we've barely been in touch for the last ten, and suddenly you fly six thousand miles and you're all over me like a rash. Why are you here? What do you want?

RUTH sits on the bank and throws bits of grass and twigs in the stream as she talks.

RUTH: When we were little, I used to think the world of you. Even though you were my younger sister – I so wanted to be like you. You were fun, you were more vivacious than me, you had so many friends. All I ever seemed to be was in the way.

GRACE: Is that why you pinched all my boyfriends?

RUTH: I did no such thing.

GRACE: Yes you did. They came to see me and ended up kissing you in the shed.

RUTH: Once. That happened once.

GRACE: Twice. Gavin Pritchard and Willy Crowe.

RUTH: Willy Crowe?

GRACE: Willy told me he fondled your breast.

RUTH: Well, he was lying.

GRACE: Really?

RUTH: Yes.

GRACE: Damn. I let him fondle both of mine to go one better.

RUTH: You didn't have any breasts.

GRACE: That's what Willy said. He said two of mine were worth one of yours so in he went with all palms blazing.

RUTH laughs. GRACE smiles and watches as RUTH dips her hand in the water and dabs her face and neck. Then...

RUTH: Grace, I'm here because I have something to tell you.

Pause.

GRACE: Well?

RUTH: You keep asking me why I've flown all this way and you're right, it isn't just to be with you. I mean, I wanted to be with you, of course I did, but there's something I want you to know.

Pause. RUTH takes a deep breath. GRACE becomes impatient.

GRACE: Oh come on, do spit it out – what?

RUTH: I have a son.

Silence as GRACE tries to take this in.

GRACE: What?

RUTH: He's called Jeremy.

GRACE: Jeremy?

RUTH: Yes.

GRACE: You have a son called Jeremy?

RUTH: Yes.

Pause.

GRACE: That's a terrible name, Ruth.

RUTH: Well, I liked it.

GRACE: For heaven's sake, what have you been up to? How old is he, this boy?

RUTH: Thirty. He's thirty years old.

GRACE: Thirty? This happened thirty years ago?... (*Grinning mischievously.*) ... Why didn't you tell me?

RUTH: It's why I went abroad.

GRACE: You mean it happened over here?

RUTH: No, he was born over there.

GRACE: Yes, yes, I've gathered that, but the business-end of things. You got pregnant over here?

RUTH: Yes.

GRACE: I don't remember you having any dalliances.

RUTH: No.

GRACE: So... So who's was it? Who's the father?

RUTH struggles, takes an even deeper breath and then looks GRACE in the eye...

RUTH: Bardy.

Pause. GRACE looks at her in disbelief.

I'm sorry Grace. For years, I've been dreading this moment. I wondered if it could somehow be avoided, but with Bardy dying... I don't know, I just felt that if I could tell you, if I could explain the whole thing, you would understand and it could all be laid to rest.

GRACE just stares at her. She looks as though she is about to speak, but no words come out.

We weren't lovers or anything, it was just a moment of madness, nothing more, and my fault entirely. You mustn't blame him.

GRACE: When?... How?... What is this, some kind of sick little joke you're playing?

RUTH: No, Grace. It's not a joke.

GRACE: I don't believe you.

RUTH: Remember when I was living in Clapham and I was trying to decide what to do with my life and I asked Bardy to come and talk to me?

GRACE: Yes, I remember it well. He came home with a plaster on his head.

RUTH: Yes. Indeed. He was so good to me, so wise and thoughtful, and when we'd finished talking he asked me if I'd like him to pray with me, and I said I would. So he did. It was such a wonderful prayer that at the end I said Amen and kissed him. Poor Bardolph, he was so shocked and confused that he tried to leave but instead he walked straight into the door. There was blood everywhere. I'll never forget it. Anyway, I told him to sit down for a minute and went to the bathroom to get a cold flannel. When I came back he was sitting in the chair with his back to me and suddenly, and for reasons I don't quite understand even to this day, I took all my clothes off. Then I asked him if he would mind unburdening me of my virginity.

GRACE: This is ridiculous. I mean, it's absurd Ruth, what are you saying to me?

RUTH: It is, I know – which is why you must know I'm not making it up.

GRACE still struggles to take it in.

He didn't want to, Grace. He resisted bravely, but I was quite determined – possessed, almost.

GRACE: No, I'm sorry, you can stop now.

RUTH: He was never unfaithful, Grace. Not in his heart.

GRACE: I said, stop it at once.

RUTH: I just hope, given time…you will come to forgive us both.

GRACE: I said, stop it! I don't know what kind of twisted pleasure you're getting from this but you can stop it right now.

RUTH: Grace…it's true.

GRACE tries to speak but can't. For a moment she looks like she might hit RUTH but she just turns and hurries off. RUTH hesitates, buries her face in her hands and then exits slowly the opposite way as the lights change swiftly to…

The garden, GRACE reappears at the greenhouse and pulls open the door…

GRACE: Bardy!… Bardolph!

BARDY appears mopping his brow with a hanky…

BARDY: Phew! Gets jolly hot in here with that door closed.

GRACE: The truth, Bardy. Is what Ruth is saying, the truth?

BARDY: Your sister is capable of many things. Whether or not telling the truth is one of them I honestly couldn't say.

GRACE: Are you or are you not the father of this child she's had?

BARDY just looks at her.

Answer me!

JO appears from the house.

JO: Sarah's gone. She said to say thank you.

GRACE: Go away.

JO: Mum?

GRACE: Go away Jo!… Bardolph! I'm talking to you.

BARDY disappears into the greenhouse.

JO: This has got to stop. You need help. I want you to see someone.

GRACE stands and weeps silently. JO goes to her and puts her arms round her.

Come here.

GRACE: It's not true. It's not true.

JO: You have to let him go now.

GRACE: I was the only one. You were the only one. He was *my* husband and *your* father, Jo, there was no one else. He never told you there was anyone else, did he?

JO: Anyone else? Of course not. What are you talking about?

GRACE: There was. There is. He's called Jeremy.

JO: Don't be ridiculous. Dad wasn't gay.

GRACE: She's evil. I want her out of this house.

JO: Want who out of this house? Mum, what are you talking about, and who the hell is Jeremy?

GRACE breaks away from JO and begins to recover herself.

GRACE: Your half brother. You have a half brother, Jo.

JO: I have a what!?

GRACE: Thirty years ago Ruth and your father made a child together and his name is Jeremy.

JO: Oh for God's sake.

GRACE: It's true.

JO: Dad and Auntie Ruth? She's a missionary, for God's sake, she doesn't do sex.

RUTH appears.

RUTH: Not often, I admit, but on the odd occasion it has been known.

RUTH and GRACE stare at each other. JO stares back and forth at both of them.

GRACE: I want you to go, Ruth. I want you to leave this house immediately.

JO: Hold on, Mum.

GRACE: You too, Jo. I'd like you both to leave me in peace.

JO: Just a minute, just a minute… How long have you known about this?

RUTH: I've just told her.

JO: What, just this second? After all these years?

RUTH: There was never going to be a good moment.

JO: Look, I'm struggling a bit. Can we just talk about this for a minute? How old was I when this happened?

RUTH: You would have been about four, Jo.

JO: Four, yes. I remember waving you off on a dockside somewhere.

RUTH: Southampton.

GRACE: Did he know you were pregnant when you left?

RUTH: I wrote to him later.

GRACE: You corresponded?

RUTH: Only briefly.

GRACE: You continued this relationship behind my back?

RUTH: No, Grace. He sent me money for the boy's upkeep and years later I sent him photos. Nothing more.

GRACE fights back tears.

He was just trying to do the responsible thing, Grace… I'll get my things and call the airline.

RUTH goes. JO turns to GRACE, approaches her but GRACE signals to her not to. JO follows RUTH off. BARDY re-appears at the greenhouse door. GRACE stares at him, distressed and angry.

GRACE: My sister? My own sister?!

BARDY: Yes.

GRACE: But...she wasn't even in the parish! Everyone knows it can happen in the parish – distraught women needing more than a shoulder to cry on – but Ruth? My sister? whatever were you thinking of?

BARDY: I wasn't thinking at all, Grace, I was in shock. It all happened so quickly, and believe me – she was quite determined.

GRACE: Oh please.

BARDY: Well, you know what your sister's like when she sets her mind to something? I was as surprised as you were, frankly – when she left the country, I mean. I never imagined...well, I thought... I *thought*...she left because of our helpful little talk.

GRACE: It *was* because of your 'helpful little talk', you fool!

BARDY: What we discussed, I mean, not...you know...that bit of silliness.

GRACE: And you never felt, you never once felt in all the years that followed, that you could tell me.

BARDY: To what end? At the time I was very ashamed, not to mention confused, and later it seemed all rather pointless.

GRACE: You had sexual intercourse with my sister, Bardy!

BARDY: It was a nasty bang on the head, old thing.

GRACE just looks at him. BARDY hangs his head.

I know. I'm sorry.

GRACE turns and walks away, leaving BARDY standing at the greenhouse door. She looks suddenly very alone.

GRACE: So cruel. This is so cruel. As if losing you the way I did weren't enough, I am left with an unfinished sentence.

BARDY: We can talk, Grace. We can talk about it now, if you like.

GRACE: No. We can't Bardy.

BARDY: Yes we can.

GRACE: We can't you stupid man, because you're not here! It's all too late! You've left it too late Bardy! You're just…not here.

GRACE sits on the ground and weeps. BARDY still watches. RUTH and JO enter from the house, RUTH stops but JO slowly steps forward towards GRACE. She crouches beside her and takes her in her arms as GRACE sobs.

JO: It's okay. It's okay.

GRACE: All those years, so many, many years of silence.

JO: I know, I know.

GRACE: Why didn't he tell me? Why didn't he tell me, Jo? My memories. All my memories…are gone.

JO holds GRACE in her arms on the ground. RUTH and BARDY watch from a distance as… The lights fade to blackout…

End of Act One

Act Two

The same. Two days later.

The sound of the lawn mower somewhere nearby. The sound recedes and then approaches again, going back and forth. As it does, GRACE wanders into the garden from the house stirring a cup in a saucer. She watches the progress of the mower off. The mower suddenly idles. RUTH enters and crosses the stage with a full grass bucket. GRACE watches as RUTH exits. GRACE stirs her coffee. RUTH re-enters with an empty grass bucket. GRACE watches her as she crosses the stage again and exits towards the idling mower. The mower revs and sets off, but then dies. RUTH re-enters and looks at GRACE who now ignores her and sips her coffee.

RUTH: What do you want me to say?

> *GRACE doesn't answer. She sips her coffee.*

Grace?

> *GRACE still doesn't respond.*

You haven't addressed a single remark to me for two days, as though you're waiting for me to say something.

> *Pause.*

I have a plane to catch this evening.

> *RUTH mops her brow and sits.*

Ask me anything you want and I'll try and give you a straight answer.

GRACE: How do you think she'll manage this garden? Without help, I mean – she's not the gardening sort at all. Does she seem the gardening sort to you?

> *RUTH stares at her. They make eye contact for the first time.*

Actually there is something I want to ask you, something that's been bothering me. Why now?

RUTH: What do you mean?

GRACE: Well. If I was in your position and had to choose a moment to tell my sister that I had a child by her husband, I don't think I'd wait until now. Would you? Well clearly you would because you did.

RUTH: It was the first opportunity.

GRACE: To do what?

RUTH: To explain.

GRACE: Explain what?

RUTH: To make sure you understood.

GRACE: Understood what?

RUTH: That Bardy wasn't to blame. I was a foolish girl who did a foolish thing. The initiative was entirely mine.

GRACE: Bardy could have told me that himself. Why didn't he?

RUTH: Because… Oh, he could have tried, Grace, yes – but thank goodness he didn't. He was far too honest for his own good and he would have turned it into a confession. He would have made out that it was somehow his fault too and I know how much that would have hurt you.

GRACE: I see. So you waited until now to make it easier.

RUTH: I suppose so, yes.

GRACE: On who?

RUTH: On you, of course.

GRACE: You do talk such utter rubbish sometimes.

RUTH: It doesn't matter what I say, does it? You're not going to hear it. Look, the truth is, my son has asked if he can meet his family. He has a right do that and that's why I've told you now. It hasn't been easy for him and he can't be expected to spend the rest of his life hidden away.

GRACE: You told me now because you couldn't live with it anymore and now that Bardy's gone you thought you'd have a stab at getting yourself off the hook.

RUTH: I am thinking of my son.

GRACE: You're thinking of yourself. What do you want – absolution? I forgive you. There. Better now? Does that help?

RUTH: Why do I have the feeling that you get some sort of pleasure from this?

GRACE: I beg your pardon?

RUTH: Ever since we were children you've done this.

GRACE: Done what?

RUTH: I've been the wicked older sister and you've played the injured party. I'd put a foot wrong and you'd run to Mummy and Daddy with some frightful story.

GRACE: Such as?

RUTH: Oh I don't know.

GRACE: Come on, such as?

RUTH: The bubble gum incident.

GRACE: What!?

RUTH: We were never allowed bubble gum, remember? It was all the rage after school but we weren't allowed it because Mummy thought it was common.

GRACE: Bubble gum?!

RUTH: Yes bubble gum. She said it was for children on the council estate who couldn't afford chocolates so they had bubble gum because it lasted longer. One day I bought some and took you into the woods to teach you how to blow bubbles. You were delighted until one exploded all over your face. You ran back to the house covered in pink rubber and I had my pocket money stopped for a month.

GRACE: I was frightened.

RUTH: Phooey! It was just another opportunity to get me into trouble. And you haven't changed. You've been in arrested development since the age of ten, Grace.

GRACE: Ruth, why don't you go home. Haven't you got a plane to catch?

RUTH: This evening, I've told you, but I was thinking of changing it.

GRACE: Well, don't. Go early, buy some duty free for your son or something.

RUTH: You'd like that wouldn't you?

GRACE: Yes. I would. Very much.

RUTH: To just leave things as they are.

GRACE: Actually I've got a better idea – Bognor. I've always liked Bognor and I could do with some sea air. Stay, go, do what you like – so long as you're gone when I get back.

GRACE makes for the house.

RUTH: Always the victim, aren't you Grace?!

GRACE turns at the door and rounds on her.

GRACE: You had sex with my husband!

RUTH: At least you had one!

This was heartfelt. RUTH is close to tears. GRACE glares at her.

GRACE: What did you say?

JO enters.

JO: Mum, I was wondering if...

GRACE pushes past her and exits into the house.

Auntie Ruth?

RUTH: Later Jo, if you don't mind.

RUTH exits the other way. JO looks despairing.

JO: Oh God.

SARAH enters from the side of the house.

Sarah?

SARAH: You said there was no need to phone.

JO: Oh. Yes... You're right, so I did.

SARAH: Is this a bad moment?

JO: No... Um... Well, yes. Things have rather erupted since you were last here. Are you okay, by the way? I was quite concerned when you left, I was even wondering whether to phone you.

SARAH: Well, I did want to have another chat.

RUTH returns from the mower. She is still distraught.

JO: Auntie Ruth I need to talk to you.

RUTH: I need to pack, Jo – I'm leaving shortly... Hello Sarah.

SARAH: Hello Ruth.

JO: Your plane isn't until tonight.

RUTH: I might also need a lift to the airport. Can you help?

JO: Of course, but I'm also concerned about Mum, Auntie Ruth.

RUTH: Yes, quite. It's no problem. I'll get a taxi.

JO: I didn't mean it like that.

SARAH: Would you like me to take you?

GRACE enters and searches round for the phone.

GRACE: Is the telephone out here? I need to call for a taxi.

SARAH: I was just saying that I could take her, if it would help?

GRACE: Take who, where?

SARAH: Your sister. To the airport.

GRACE: Take her wherever you like – the sooner the better, as far as I'm concerned – the taxi's for me.

JO: Why? Where are you going?

GRACE: To the railway station.

GRACE finds the phone and dials.

JO: What for?

GRACE: To catch a train.

JO: Why? Where are you going?

GRACE: Bognor… (*Phone.*) Yes, I'd like to order a taxi please.

SARAH: Perhaps it would be better if I left.

JO: No please don't.

GRACE: (*Phone.*) The Rectory, Farm Lane.

JO: (*To GRACE.*) Why Bognor?

GRACE: (*Phone.*) Yes, that would be fine, thank you.

GRACE ignores her and makes towards the stream.

JO: Mum, please will you just wait a minute?

GRACE: I'll be down by the stream if you want me.

RUTH: If I shared your taxi, Grace, the driver could take me on to the airport.

GRACE turns and looks at her.

GRACE: Oh no. I don't think so, Ruth. They're in opposite directions.

GRACE tosses the phone onto the table and exits. RUTH is fighting back tears. SARAH sees this and puts a reassuring arm round her. JO picks up the phone and presses re-dial.

JO: Auntie Ruth? I think you should call the airline and change your flight.

RUTH: There's no point, Jo.

JO: There's every point. You and Mum shouldn't part like this… (*Phone.*) Yes, my mother has just ordered a taxi for the Rectory, I'd like to cancel it please… Thank you.

RUTH: I'm going to finish packing.

JO: I'm going to call the airline. What's the number?

RUTH: I don't have it. It's in my room.

JO hands the phone to RUTH.

JO: Here. Go and find the number and call them. I'll find Mum and get her to abandon Bognor. Yes?

JO holds RUTH who looks broken and defeated.

This must be so hard for you.

RUTH: It had to come.

JO: We'll sort it out, I promise.

RUTH exits into the house. SARAH looks at JO who laughs despairingly.

Don't even ask.

JO flops down on a chair.

It's like *Songs of Praise* on acid here.

SARAH: Are you okay?

JO: Yes, yes. I'm fine.

JO buries her face in her hands wearily.

SARAH: No, you're not.

JO: No, I'm not.

Beat. JO becomes tearful.

God, they've got me at it now. What is it with men, Sarah?
They have this…gift…for creating chaos, and when it's too
late to do anything, they just…bugger off…leaving us to
step in and clear up the mess. (*Beat.*) You know something?
I really loved my father, I really did. I looked up to him,
I admired him, I have the best childhood memories…
And when he walked me up the aisle, he let go of my arm,
and hopped onto the altar steps and took the service…
And when he gave me away, he kissed my hand. And
later, when my marriage went down, he was so…kind and
understanding – he actually cried with me. We sat together,
right here and cried. On this bench… I miss him and I
loved him so much and… I don't think I ever told him,
Sarah. Not once.

*JO searches for a hanky. SARAH reaches into her basket and hands
her one.*

And now, it turns out, that this wonderful, super-human
father of mine may, in fact, have been a bit of a prick.

SARAH: What do you mean?

JO: My dear batty aunt…has just revealed…that my late
departed Dad…had a thing with her.

SARAH: A thing?

JO: Yes, a thing.

SARAH: Ruth?

JO: Auntie Ruth… And my father.

SARAH: Oh my God!

JO: I'm trying to get to the bottom of it, but neither of them will occupy the same room. Oh, and there's a son. Called Jeremy. Did I mention that?

SARAH: No.

JO: Well, there is.

SARAH: She got pregnant?

JO: That's the traditional way of acquiring one. He's thirty and he lives in africa. Actually, I'm not sure if I should be telling you all this. Should I be telling you this?

SARAH: It's fine, and a bit late now anyway. Besides, I do...

JO & SARAH: ... Do it for a living.

JO: ... Yes, I know. But it puts you in a weird position for the future, doesn't it?

SARAH: Why?

JO: For a start, no one else in the parish knows.

SARAH: Ah. Well. That may not be a problem now.

JO: What do you mean?

SARAH: I don't think I'm taking the job, after all.

JO: Oh for God's sake Sarah!

SARAH: I talked it over with Nicholas and I'm seeing the bishop tomorrow, like you said. I don't think I'm ready. That's why I came to see you, and also to tell your mother. There are things I have to resolve, Jo.

JO: Such as?

SARAH: I really don't want to go into it.

JO: You had an affair. It was the catalyst for your faith. What is there to resolve?

Pause. SARAH looks awkward.

Look, I don't want to pry but I don't want you making a wrong decision because of something I said… Sarah?

SARAH: I had a termination, Jo.

Beat.

JO: What?… When?

SARAH: When Nicholas and I put our lives back together, I fell pregnant. We had the twelve week scan, and there was no heart beat, so…

JO: So… What?… You feel guilt?

SARAH: Not about the termination. We had no choice.

JO: What then?

Beat.

SARAH: Nick wasn't the father.

JO: Ah… Hamish?

SARAH nods… She struggles to get the words out.

SARAH: And I never told him. I watched my husband grieve over a child that wasn't his. And I was relieved.

Pause. JO looks toward the arch to the stream.

JO: Look… Um…do me a favour, will you? While I go and find my mother, will you stay here and keep an eye on Ruth?

SARAH: Haven't you got enough on your plate?

JO: Yes. I have – without Auntie Ruth topping herself in the bathroom, so do this one thing for me, will you?

SARAH: Yes. Of course.

JO: We'll talk more in a while.

JO hurries off toward the stream.

Sound of rushing water. BARDY appears by the stream as GRACE enters. BARDY is making notes and scribbling in his book. GRACE stands and watches him in silence. After a pause…

GRACE: When I met you, the first thing I noticed was that you had long thin legs and a completely shapeless torso. I remember thinking, 'Oh no. He won't do at all. I haven't waited all these years to be de-flowered by a stick insect.' No, no what I had in mind was Rock Hudson in a dog collar.

Pause. BARDY is still scribbling.

BARDY: Wasn't he a homosexual?

GRACE: Mmmh?

BARDY: Rock Hudson.

GRACE: Was he?

BARDY: (*Still scribbling.*) I think I read it somewhere.

GRACE: Well, they all were, weren't they.

BARDY: Mind you, he was in that marvellous film, whatever was it?

GRACE: I've no idea, and anyway that's not the point…

BARDY: Yes you do. Doris day was in it.

GRACE: … The point is, clergy daughter or no, I was entitled to believe that my virginity would be entrusted to the hands of an Adonis with a firm bottom…not a bean pole in aertex y-fronts.

Pause. BARDY looks up from his notes.

BARDY: *Pillow Talk.*

GRACE: What?

BARDY: That film he was in. We saw it at the Regal.

GRACE: The Regal? What, before it was pulled down.

BARDY returns to his writing.

BARDY: Presumably, yes.

GRACE: You're missing my point again, Bardy.

BARDY: Am I? I'm so sorry. Your point being?

GRACE: My point being that it didn't really matter what your body was like because it was your mind that I fell in love with. Nature is very clever like that, it can only happen that way round.

BARDY: What way round?

GRACE: If you like the way someone looks, you won't necessarily fall in love with their mind, but if you love someone's mind you will almost certainly come to love their body.

BARDY: Very profound, old thing.

GRACE: Just as well, really. You only spend a few hours a day with someone's body – and that's mostly in the dark – but you spend the whole of your life with their mind.

BARDY: So long as they don't go gah-gah.

GRACE: Well quite. Are you thinking of going gah-gah?

BARDY: It's not in the diary, no. Not until they make me a bishop… (*Chuckling at his own joke.*) … Ha! and then it's a pre-requisite!

GRACE laughs with him. She nestles up to him.

GRACE: I do love you, Bardy.

BARDY: I love you too, old thing.

GRACE: Make love to me.

BARDY continues writing.

BARDY: One second while I just get this down.

GRACE: Bardy?

BARDY: (*Still writing.*) Mmmh?

GRACE: Remember how we used to, down here by the stream?

BARDY: (*Finishing.*) Right. Sorry. I'm all ears. What were you saying?

JO enters.

JO: I've cancelled your taxi.

BARDY wanders off. GRACE watches him.

Why Bognor?

GRACE: It's where we had our honeymoon.

GRACE wanders over to the tree.

This stream has so many memories. A thousand conversations. You were conceived down here you know? more or less where I'm standing now.

JO: Thank you, Mother – a little too much information.

GRACE: One of his better sermons I seem to recall – largely because it was so short.

JO: Look, I think I've persuaded Auntie Ruth to postpone her flight. I have no idea how to go about this but you and she, all three of us in fact, have to try and work something out.

GRACE: It's too late, Jo.

JO: No it isn't.

GRACE: His son, your half brother, is walking around Africa.

JO: It was a long time ago.

GRACE: And it happened during the years that I loved him most. Then he began to disappear. The church became his wife and I was just the woman he slept with. I never knew why.

JO: He loved you.

GRACE: Yes, I think he did.

JO: And you loved him.

GRACE: Yes I most certainly did.

JO: Then let him go, let him rest.

JO goes to her and holds her. She glances down to the stream.

Mister Whiskers is back.

GRACE: Mmmh?

JO: The water rat. Sarah saw him the other day… Will you do that? Will you come with me and find Auntie Ruth? She's your sister, she's in a terrible state.

GRACE looks at her and strokes her face.

GRACE: He loved you too – so very much.

JO: I know. I know he did.

GRACE: You have such a look of him about you sometimes… (*Kisses JO's forehead.*) You go ahead. I'll join you shortly.

JO: Thank you.

JO exits one way while GRACE wanders off the other way. Sound of water crescendos then recedes altogether.

Back in the garden, SARAH waits. RUTH appears from the house, looking at a piece of paper with flight times scribbled on it.

RUTH: I called the airline, Jo… Oh.

SARAH: She's down by the stream.

RUTH: Right. Thank you. More measuring?

SARAH: Sorry?… No. Just visiting.

RUTH: You picked the right day for it.

SARAH: Yes. It's beautiful.

RUTH: I wasn't referring to the weather.

SARAH: Ah. No.

RUTH: Poor you. Walked into a bit of a do, I'm afraid. Fear not, we'll have washed the blood off the walls by the time you arrive.

SARAH: Look…Ruth…the last thing I want to do is interfere.

RUTH: No, quite.

Awkward pause. RUTH studies her notes. SARAH searches for something to say.

SARAH: Must be a busy life being a missionary.

RUTH: Oh… The usual stuff. AIDS, abortion and domestic carnage, nothing fancy. The famines and genocide most people read about in the Sunday papers are my average day at the office.

SARAH: Yes… I have friends… I do know what you're talking about.

RUTH: Yes, I'm sure. I didn't mean to be rude. Look, I'm sorry about the histrionics earlier. I made a bit of an ass of myself.

SARAH: Wonderful creatures, asses.

RUTH: Are they?

SARAH: Yes. Traditionally they are creatures of idiotic stubbornness but people seem to forget that they were there at the birth and Christ made his triumphal entry into Jerusalem on one at the end.

Beat.

RUTH: You'll fit in here splendidly. When is it you move in?

SARAH: Oh… I'm not sure.

RUTH: I thought it was quite soon.

SARAH: Nothing's set in stone.

RUTH: I thought everything in the Church of England was set in stone, I thought that was rather its problem.

SARAH: Yes, quite. No, the truth is… I may not be taking the position at all.

RUTH: Oh. Why not?

SARAH: Personal reasons.

RUTH: I love that expression. I used it all the time when I fled the country. It covers a multitude of sins.

SARAH: Ha! Which of yours did it cover?

RUTH: Hasn't Jo told you?

SARAH: Oh!… Yes… I'm sorry. Golly, how tactless. I'm so sorry.

RUTH: Nonsense. So come on, your turn – it's dirty linen day, a bit more won't hurt.

JO enters from the stream…

JO: Mum's on her way…

SARAH: Good. Right. I think I'd better be going.

JO: Why don't you come back a bit later, Sarah?

SARAH: No, really. I'll phone you or something.

JO: Just promise me you won't do anything hasty – not until we've talked.

SARAH gets her bag and turns to go.

Sarah?… My father would have liked you, you know. I…just wanted you to know that.

SARAH acknowledges with a smile.

SARAH: Bye Ruth. I hope…everything…you know… Bye.

SARAH goes.

JO: Poor thing.

RUTH: She said she might not be coming here – has she got cold feet or something?

JO: Something like that. All frightfully complicated.

JO sits on the bench and leans her head back.

Oh God! Relationships, Auntie Ruth! Why can't they be simple?

RUTH: Probably because they wouldn't be relationships if they were. Like cars, I always think – costly to run, go wrong when you least expect and in constant need of a good service. What happened to yours Jo, you don't talk about it much?

RUTH sits next to her.

JO: Oh… He was an idiot.

RUTH: Did you love him?

JO: I thought so. I told myself I did.

RUTH: If you had to tell yourself, then clearly you didn't, so why did you marry him?

JO: I liked him, everyone liked him, it seemed sensible, lots of ticks in lots of boxes. Oh, it's no good asking me now. The man's a pillock. The end.

RUTH: Why, oh why, do women marry men they don't love?

JO: God knows, but I've had it with all of them. Could you convert me and then I can come and do worthy things with you in Africa?

RUTH: Now that would be fun.

JO: We'd have a blast. You, me and my new half brother could live saintly lives during the day and get rat-arsed every night.

Pause as JO ponders RUTH's earlier question.

Women marry men they don't love to protect themselves – from being hurt.

RUTH: If that's true, it's very sad.

JO: Well, isn't it? To love someone is the most dangerous thing you can do – if you don't love them, you're safe. Most of the couples I see don't even like each other – if they weren't actually married, they wouldn't even be friends.

RUTH: So there you are fixing other people's marriages while your own goes down the plug.

JO: Oh, yes. I'm hot stuff when it comes to other people.

RUTH: And you never saw it coming?

JO: Probably, but communication was never our strong point – it's our family failing, isn't it?

RUTH: For a family, I think we talk quite alot.

JO: Oh we talk endlessly, Dad was famous for it but no one ever actually communicates. We speak in statements, but there's no engagement.

RUTH gives her an affectionate squeeze.

RUTH: Well…we're not doing too badly.

JO: No, we're not. I would like to feel safe with someone – someone I loved. I just don't want to take risks anymore.

RUTH: Life is all about risk, Jo – what matters is who you take them with.

Brief pause. JO looks up at RUTH.

JO: Did you love him?

RUTH: From a distance, yes very much. But only from a distance, Jo. What happened between your father and me...

GRACE enters. RUTH and JO cuddled on the bench quickly disengage.

JO: Ah. You're here. Good.

GRACE: Yes. I'm here.

RUTH: Jo has persuaded me to postpone my flight, Grace.

GRACE: I know.

RUTH: Until we've talked.

GRACE: I'm listening. What do you want to say?

JO: Look, I'm not sure if I should be here for this. I mean, I will if it helps and I'd like to know more but...

GRACE: I'm happy for her to be here. Are you happy for her to be here, Ruth?

RUTH: Yes, I'm happy for her to be here. I've nothing to hide.

GRACE: Ha!

RUTH: I've tried to be honest, Grace, and to make my position open and clear.

GRACE: Oh, enlighten us, do, on the missionary position, Ruth!

RUTH: No, I'm sorry but I'm not going to sit here and be insulted like this.

GRACE: Then bugger off back to Africa!

RUTH: Yes, and you can bugger off to Bognor!

JO: Oh, for God's sake, both of you!

They both look at her slightly taken aback.

No one's pretending this is easy but can you please at least make an effort to act your age. Sit down, the pair of you.

Neither of them move.

Now!

They both obey.

Now look, if you do want me here I reserve the right to ask what I like. All right?... Auntie Ruth?

RUTH: Of course, dear. Ask away.

JO: Mum?

GRACE: Fine. By the way, who are you going to invoice for this?

JO: Mum, please... You have a son called Jeremy, Auntie Ruth, is that right?

RUTH: Yes.

JO: And he and I share the same father.

Pause. RUTH looks at GRACE.

RUTH: Yes.

JO: (*To GRACE.*) And Dad never mentioned this to you in all the years you were married?

GRACE: No.

JO: So now he's gone and we're left to pick up the pieces. Great, thanks Dad.

GRACE: Don't speak about your father like that.

JO: Well, honestly.

GRACE: He was your father. He still is, and I'll thank you to show some respect.

JO: It's a mess, Mum. He might have guessed this would happen and made some provision for it.

RUTH: By doing what, Jo?

JO: I don't know. Written Mum a letter?

GRACE: Saying what? 'My darling Grace, sorry to have died on you. PS, I had sex with your sister and we have a son.'?

JO: At least it would have been honest.

GRACE: There's nothing honest about any of this, especially coming from her – so don't be taken in by anything that woman says.

RUTH: I'm not listening to this.

GRACE: Listening to what – the truth?

RUTH: No, this! You! Grace the victim, Grace the martyr. You insult people, you think it's funny. You patronise them, you think it's clever. You're a bully – that's all you are – a playground bully in a tweed skirt.

GRACE: Am I!

RUTH: Yes!

GRACE: And you – masquerading as this caring Christian, always ready with a helping hand. You're an adulteress! The only thing you help is yourself – to other people's husbands!

JO: Okay… Okay…

RUTH: I've had just about a bellyful of this.

GRACE: You had a bellyful of my husband, you can have a bellyful of me.

JO: Oh, please! Both of you! Stop it, now!… Dear God. Can we please, at least try, and maintain some kind of dignity?

GRACE: The only dignified thing about your aunt's life will be her tombstone.

JO: That's enough!

Pause.

Auntie Ruth?

RUTH: Yes dear.

JO: My half brother, Jeremy.

RUTH: Yes dear.

JO: Does he…well… Does he look like Dad?

GRACE: Good question. You never know – he could have one of a dozen fathers.

JO: I said – enough!

GRACE: It might even be worth checking his colour.

JO: Stop it!… Auntie Ruth?

RUTH: Sometimes. From certain angles you catch an expression.

JO: I'd like to meet him. (*To GRACE.*) Would that upset you?

GRACE: Up to you. He's your half brother.

JO: That's not what I asked.

GRACE: Look, I don't really see the point in this. What's done is done. Ruth has a son, you have a brother, and Bardy's dead.

RUTH: Your father was not to blame, Jo. You must understand that.

JO: This isn't about blame. It's about the truth, what happened, facing it and living with it.

GRACE: We know what happened. She's already told me.

JO: Well, I don't. No one's actually told me.

GRACE: There's not much to tell, is there Ruth? Many years ago she summoned your father to her bed-sit for advice. He went, said a prayer, she kissed him, and he stood up and banged his head… At which point she did what any reasonable person would do under the circumstances – she took her clothes off and had sex with him.

JO looks at her mother astonished, then slowly turns to RUTH awaiting some kind of protest. None comes. RUTH just shrugs in agreement.

RUTH: More or less.

JO: He banged his head!?

RUTH: He was confused. It wasn't his fault.

JO struggles not to laugh.

JO: I'm sorry, I'm sorry. So…there wasn't a relationship, you weren't having an affair or anything.

RUTH: Good heavens no! He was my brother-in-law. What do you take me for!?

JO: So, it was just a one-night stand.

GRACE: An afternoon stand if my memory serves me, he was back in time for harvest supper.

JO cannot contain her laughter anymore. RUTH and GRACE watch her expressionless.

JO: I'm sorry, I don't mean to laugh…it's just… I do love you both, you know that?

JO laughs out loud again. SARAH returns.

SARAH: It's nice to hear some merriment. Sorry to disturb you but I seem to have lost my car keys – yet again.

JO: (*Still recovering.*) Oh dear. Have you?

SARAH searches round. RUTH and GRACE just stare at her.

SARAH: Always doing it, drives Nicholas mad… Ah, there they are. What an idiot. So sorry. I'll leave you in peace.

GRACE: *Pax vobiscum.*

SARAH: Yes – and you, Mrs Thomas.

GRACE: Actually Sarah, you might find this rather interesting.

JO: Er… No Mother, I don't think so.

GRACE: Here's the situation, Sarah. It transpires that my late husband…

JO: Mum, what are you doing?

GRACE: I'm giving Sarah an opportunity to test drive her pastoral skills.

JO: Ignore her. Don't let us keep you.

GRACE: … It transpires that my late husband once fathered a child by my sister here.

SARAH: Yes, she did tell me.

GRACE: Did she? Oh good. So you're generally up to speed then. Well, what my daughter now finds so amusing was that 'it' – that is to say the act of sexual intimacy – only happened once and therefore, in her opinion, was of no real significance. What do you think?

RUTH: Grace, this is quite inappropriate.

GRACE: Is it? Dear me. That will never do. Let's not have anyone do anything inappropriate – but let's all just roger who we like!

RUTH: (*To GRACE.*) You're just cheapening it, Grace!

GRACE: (*To RUTH.*) You seduced my husband!

RUTH: Yes, I did! And it was wrong and stupid and I did everything possible to keep you from knowing!

GRACE: What do you want me to do – thank you!?

An embarrassed silence. Even JO is at a loss.

So Sarah, perhaps you'd like to share your thoughts with us?

JO: Honestly. Don't get dragged into this.

GRACE: Let her have her say, Jo.

JO: About what? The bottom line is – nothing happened.

GRACE: Oh you think so?

JO: Well, did it? Tell me – what?

GRACE: Betrayal?

JO: What, because he once had sex with Auntie Ruth?

GRACE: No, Jo. *Not* because he 'once had sex with Auntie Ruth.'

JO: Well, what then?

Beat.

SARAH: Because he never told her… Am I right, Mrs Thomas?

GRACE's silence says everything.

'A time to speak and a time to be silent.' I'm sure that whatever he did, he did it to protect you.

GRACE: Protect me or protect himself?

SARAH: Perhaps both.

GRACE: Perhaps neither. I think he just hid. And he stayed in hiding for the rest of his life.

SARAH: Hiding from who, Mrs Thomas?

GRACE: God, probably. I don't know. Anyway, full marks for pastoral skills, Sarah. Thank you, you've done marvellously. Can we leave this now?

JO: Why were you so angry with him?

GRACE: I've asked if we can leave this now.

GRACE gets up to leave.

(*To RUTH.*) Talk to her about your son, show her some pictures or something. I'm going for a walk.

JO: You can't keep running away, Mum.

GRACE: I'm not running away from anything, how dare you accuse me of running away.

SARAH: Mrs Thomas, at the risk of speaking out of turn, can I ask you a delicate question?

GRACE is silent. Merely waits for the question.

You spoke to me the other day about the importance of having a family.

GRACE: I did.

SARAH: And a large one, at that.

GRACE: Yes.

SARAH: You only had one child.

GRACE: What's your point?

SARAH: Well… I suppose… I was wondering why. Did you want more?

GRACE: Yes.

GRACE sees SARAH and JO waiting. They sense there is more.

But I lost one.

JO: You never told me that.

GRACE: (*To SARAH.*) Then the moment passed and he lost interest – I think we had an organ appeal or something. Does that answer your question?

JO: How late in the pregnancy were you?

GRACE: Twenty weeks. He was a little boy. I really must insist that we stop this now.

JO: So, I had a brother.

GRACE: Yes, you had a brother. You were about four at the time.

JO: Four?… So… While Auntie Ruth was in Africa carrying Dad's child…

GRACE: Yes! I was losing his other child here. Ironic, isn't it? The almighty has a strange sense of justice sometimes.

RUTH: Grace. I am so sorry.

GRACE: Don't patronise me with your apologies, you wicked woman.

JO: That's not fair, Mum.

GRACE: Fair? You talk to me about fair?! She knew!…
(*To RUTH.*) You knew, didn't you?

RUTH doesn't answer.

Didn't you?!

RUTH: Yes. He wrote to me. He was devastated. He felt…

GRACE: Felt what? What did he feel, Ruth?

RUTH: He felt it was a judgement.

GRACE: On who for God's sake?! I was the one mourning a dead child.

JO: He was the father, Mum.

GRACE: So he was, how silly of me. But he was all right, wasn't he? He had a spare in the boot, one in reserve.

JO: Oh come on.

GRACE: (*To RUTH.*) You really are the most loathesome creature.

RUTH: I can't re-write the past, Grace.

GRACE: No but having stolen mine, you might at least have had the decency to own up to it.

JO: That's what she's trying to do, Mum.

GRACE: You don't know what your talking about, Jo – none of you do. You think this is about her? This isn't about her. (*To RUTH.*) When Bardy wrote to you with his tragic news, Ruth, how did you reply?

RUTH: I told him that as a man of God he should know better. That God's capacity to judge was in equal measure to his capacity to forgive.

GRACE: Comforting words, wouldn't you say, Sarah?

SARAH: Well… Yes, if the Grace of God means anything at all I believe it affords us hope, certainly – hope that we can live on in spite of our mistakes.

GRACE: In other words – forget all about it and carry on.

SARAH: Sometimes God allows us to forget.

GRACE: Does he. How magnanimous. She didn't forget, did she?

RUTH: How could I? I had a son to remind me.

GRACE: Lucky you!

Pause. GRACE fights back emotion. JO goes to her, but GRACE pushes her away.

It isn't that he weakened or that he committed an indiscretion – for God's sake, I wasn't born yesterday, I know it can happen, I've seen it happen – I'm a clergy wife. And it isn't even that he did it with you, Ruth. What hurts…so much…and what I cannot forgive him for…is that he never told me.

SARAH: Forgiveness…is an act of will, Mrs Thomas.

GRACE: Yes, but you have to know first, don't you? You have to be given the chance. Someone has to take a risk and tell. Isn't that what confession is all about – taking a risk with the truth?

SARAH: Maybe he felt that you would be too damaged. Destroyed, even.

GRACE: By the truth? Oh, where is your faith, young woman? no one gets damaged by the truth, it's lies that damage and destroy. Anyway, if you're right, and he thought that our love for each other might not be strong enough to sustain it – then that is an even deeper wound…the worst insult of all…and one I certainly cannot forgive him for. Maybe God can, maybe he has – but there, I'm afraid, God and I have to part company.

SARAH: Perhaps he was just too ashamed.

GRACE: No doubt, but he went to God for forgiveness, didn't he – not me.

SARAH: Then maybe it was the only way he knew of putting it behind him.

GRACE: Oh yes. Nothing like a bit of divine absolution for getting yourself off the hook. No, the truth is, my husband…who I loved so very deeply…was a coward.

JO: He was a good man – and to me, he was everything, you know that.

GRACE: Oh yes. I knew that only too well.

JO: He was just another person blundering about in the dark.

GRACE: *Hiding* in the dark, Jo. He was a theologian and he should have known…that at the heart of everything he believed…was something called grace. But that takes courage, which he didn't have, so instead he just hid behind his theology. He was a man of God, and I had to watch as his theology destroyed him…without ever knowing why. I watched as he used it, not to get closer to God, but to hide from him…and himself…and me. The sad old man who died by the stream was a corpse long before he drowned.

Pause. GRACE is overcome. JO approaches her mother.

JO: No, Mum – he didn't drown. He died of heart failure.

GRACE: No, he didn't.

JO: Yes. He did.

GRACE: I should know. I was there.

JO: What do you mean? You told me yourself, you found him in the water and it was too late.

GRACE: I lied.

JO: The death certificate said heart failure, what are you saying?

Pause. GRACE stares at her... Then turns and leaves.

Sudden light change, sound of rushing water. RUTH, JO and SARAH remain barely visible on the patio in the background, as GRACE re-lives the scene by the stream...

BARDY enters making notes on his notepad. He leans against the tree by the bank of the stream, scribbling away. GRACE re-enters. She watches him for a moment.

GRACE: Are you feeling better?

BARDY: Yes, yes. It was nothing.

GRACE: That's not what the doctor told me.

BARDY: When the time comes, the time comes. It's all in the grand plan. Listen to this, I've got an idea for Sunday evensong.

GRACE: Oh God.

BARDY: No, it's rather to the point. The almighty is never without a plan. As early as Genesis we read that first he made the perfect place, then he made a perfect creature then he gave him a perfect partner. Now then...

GRACE: That's nonsense.

BARDY: I beg your pardon?

GRACE: It wasn't a perfect plan, Bardy it was a muddle. First he formed the heavens and the earth then he formed a man and then he realised – what? That 'it wasn't good for Adam to be alone' and something was missing.

BARDY: Yes. So he created Eve.

GRACE: No he didn't, he wheeled in the animals. Adam sat there naming them all until the poor bugger was yawning his head off. The almighty was hovering about scratching his head, and what do the scriptures say next?

BARDY: 'But there was not found a helper fit for him.'

GRACE: Exactly. The almighty tried a string of ideas but none of them worked, in other words he was busking it.

BARDY: He found the answer in the end though.

GRACE: A woman. Yes, he got there eventually, bless him. But it was a hell of a long way round. If he'd been quicker off the mark we wouldn't have any animals at all.

BARDY: Grace dear, I'm wondering if what you're saying might be blasphemy.

GRACE: Burn me at the stake then. There isn't a plan, Bardy – the whole thing was, and still is, a divine exercise in trial and error.

BARDY: Are you having a crisis of faith, old thing?

GRACE laughs despairingly.

GRACE: Faith in what?

BARDY: In God.

GRACE: Which one? He's become a chameleon. The grand puppeteer who pulls the strings and fixes our lives? No, I don't believe in him anymore.

BARDY: What about the one who loves you?

GRACE: Yes I believe in him, but so does the fanatic that flies planes into tall buildings.

BARDY: Now you're being ridiculous.

GRACE: (*Exploding.*) I am not being ridiculous! Don't you dare stand there and tell me I'm being ridiculous!

BARDY looks shaken by this outburst. GRACE recovers herself.

You used to laugh. You had a brilliant mind and upset people at dinner parties. Where have you been, Bardy?

BARDY: Here, Grace. What do you mean?

GRACE: You're my husband and I haven't seen you for thirty years.

BARDY: Where do you suppose I have been then?

GRACE: Playing with God, still naming the animals? I don't know. I want the two people who set out together to finish the journey. Is that so much to ask?

BARDY goes to her.

BARDY: You want me to give up the parish. Is that it?

GRACE: I want you to come out of hiding so I can live with the man I married.

BARDY: Hiding?

GRACE: Or prison perhaps. I don't know. Your faith has become a religion, Bardy. God has become your jailor.

BARDY: Oh now…! Well, of course, in many ways, you're right. We are all prisoners of his love.

GRACE: Oh for God's sake.

BARDY: What have I said now?

GRACE: You're not listening to me. It's a nice phrase but you don't seriously mean that, do you?

BARDY: Yes. Yes I do. I am captive to the love of God but, like you, like all of us, I hold the keys to my own cell.

Pause. GRACE just looks at him. BARDY reaches for his notebook.

Actually, that's rather good, I must write that...

GRACE snatches the notebook from him.

GRACE: Speak to me Bardy!

BARDY: About what, Grace?

GRACE: About whatever it is you are hiding from.

BARDY: I'm not hiding, I'm not hiding from anything. Why do you keep saying that?

Beat.

GRACE: Because of your silence.

BARDY looks at her long and hard, as though he is about speak... But no words come out and he remains silent.

Ask him to set you free, Bardy. Please? Or better still, if you really hold the keys to your own cell, in God's name set yourself free.

BARDY: I can't, Grace. It's not possible.

BARDY goes to her...

If a loving God is, as you say, my jailor, then yes... I choose my prison.

GRACE looks at him, at a loss. BARDY smiles kindly and kisses her on the cheek...and gently takes his notebook back.

Now, if you don't mind, I really must get on and finish...

BARDY suddenly stumbles, and almost falls.

GRACE: Bardy?

BARDY: I'm all right.

He stumbles again and leans against the tree, struggling for breath. She goes to help him but he waves her away.

I'm all right, I tell you.

BARDY slips to the ground and slides down the bank away from us and disappears towards the stream.

GRACE: Bardy!

A single light picks out GRACE kneeling by the stream. BARDY has gone.

I got down into the stream but he was too heavy to lift, so I sat in the water beside him… And held his head. I cradled it for a moment while he fought for breath. I tried to loosen his collar but I couldn't undo the stud. Then he went still. I felt numb and instead of raising his head, I gently lowered it into the water… And held it there, beneath the surface. Almost like a baptism. It seemed a simple choice – to either raise him up or hold him down. He didn't struggle. He seemed to let me.

RUTH and JO stare at GRACE without moving. GRACE looks back at them helplessly…appealing for something.

I wanted to set him free. That's all… Oh!… What did I do? What have I done?

RUTH: Nothing. It's all right. You haven't done anything.

GRACE: I have, I have.

JO: No. Mum. Listen to me. The head you held down in the water had already gone. It was heart failure, the doctor told me.

RUTH: It was his time, Grace. That's all.

GRACE: If only he had told me. Why didn't he tell me?

GRACE sobs. RUTH glances at JO. It is enough for JO to know that RUTH wants to be alone with her sister. JO and SARAH exit into the house together. RUTH looks at her broken sister.

RUTH: He wanted to, Grace. He wanted to tell you…so much.

GRACE: Then why didn't he? I would have understood. If he had told me, he might even be here now.

RUTH: No. He wouldn't. And he didn't tell you for all those years…because I told him not to.

GRACE turns and looks at her.

It was my fault. I begged him not to.

GRACE: Why?… Why!?

RUTH: I told him…that if he did, he would lose you.

GRACE: But…that wasn't true.

RUTH: I know.

GRACE: Then why did you do it?

RUTH struggles with her tears.

RUTH: I think…it was to protect myself. I told myself it was to protect you, but that was a lie. I was simply trying to protect myself.

GRACE looks at her, trying to understand.

I was afraid, I was always afraid of your disapproval. I think Bardy and I were both in hiding – not from God's anger but yours.

The two women stand and look at each other. They are both weeping silently.

What I did to you, was unforgivable. But *I* did it…not Bardy.

GRACE raises her eyes to RUTH.

You are my sister, and I love you. I'm sorry.

GRACE slowly raises her hands to RUTH. Awkwardly, they move together and hold each other.

I'm sorry… I'm sorry… I'm sorry.

GRACE and RUTH embrace and weep together for a moment… As the lights slowly fade on them.

Beat.

The lights come up on the garden again as SARAH enters from the house in a long black cassock. She waddles about, heavily pregnant, whilst on her mobile phone.

SARAH: (*Phone.*) Not really, can't you do it Nick?… No, I've got a funeral at twelve, a working lunch with the dean, then back here for a marriage preparation, then I have to get ready for the 'who's hiding from who?' group tonight… No, you don't have to cook, just get a pizza we can slam in the oven… Oh anything with anchovies – and I'm out of ice cream, by the way… Yes, fine… What?… Of course I am – apart from chronic heart-burn and swollen ankles, I'm fine… Yes, I love you too.

As SARAH slips the mobile into her cassock pocket she finds a packet of sweets. She tucks into them whilst struggling to make herself comfortable on the bench. The house phone rings. She attempts to get up but it's too much effort.

Go away!… Go away!… (*Pleading heavenward.*) … Five minutes? Is that so much to ask?…(*Phone stops.*) Thank you.

She reclines on the bench and shuts her eyes sucking on her sweets.

Beat.

GRACE wanders on from the side entrance. She watches SARAH for a few seconds…

GRACE: Hail, oh favoured one.

SARAH: (*Almost choking.*) Oh, my goodness!… Mrs Thomas? You gave me the fright of my life.

GRACE: Sorry, did you think I was a visitation?

SARAH: Ha! Hardly, no… I mean – no, not at all. I was just…

GRACE: Forgive me, I've disturbed your little nap. I would have phoned but as I was passing...

SARAH gets up.

SARAH: Of course. I'm delighted. Heavens. It has been a while.

GRACE: (*Seeing SARAH's condition.*) ... Yes. I haven't had a chance to congratulate you.

SARAH: Thank you. Seven weeks to go. Keeping going to the last minute, hopefully. Well, what a nice surprise. I catch sight of you occasionally at the back of the church.

GRACE: Yes, I like to slip away, I hope you don't mind.

Brief pause.

SARAH: Not at all, I quite understand. So... Was there something you wanted or was it just a social call?

GRACE: Neither really. Well, it's nice to see you obviously but...um... I was wondering if I could just sit for a while.

SARAH: Sit?

GRACE: Yes.

SARAH: Are you unwell? Can I get you something?

GRACE: No, nothing like that. I just wondered if I could be alone...only for a minute or two.

SARAH: Out here in the garden?

GRACE: Would that be all right?

SARAH: Of course, of course. You should see the stream, Nick has done wonders down there – Bardy's dam, he calls it.

GRACE: Really.

SARAH: Full of trout and breeding like stink. Babies swimming about everywhere.

GRACE: Well. Unfortunately I haven't time for that, but I'll take a few minutes here, if you don't mind.

SARAH: Of course, help yourself… (*GRACE already has.*) You're sure I can't get you anything?

GRACE: No, no. I'll be fine.

SARAH: Right. Well. Take as long as you like… Very nice to see you, Mrs Thomas.

GRACE: Very nice to see you too.

SARAH: I'll be inside if you need anything.

SARAH goes. As GRACE takes in her old surroundings, BARDY appears. He stands framed in the arbor, smartly dressed in a suit and tie, no panama, hair brushed.

BARDY: How's the new place?

GRACE turns and looks at him.

GRACE: Small. It's packed to the gunnels, half my things don't fit, and yet it's strangely empty. It's as good a place as any to die in.

BARDY: You're not waiting to die, Grace. Far too much to do.

GRACE: Not waiting to die just wandering about.

BARDY: The Israelites wandered for forty years in the wilderness.

GRACE: Only because there were men in charge and they wouldn't stop and ask directions.

BARDY smiles. She smiles back at him.

I dreamt about you last night.

BARDY: Yes, I know.

GRACE: It was so vivid, so clear, and I thought… I don't know… I thought I'd like to come here and see you one last time.

BARDY: I'm glad.

Brief pause.

GRACE: I wish you had told me, Bardy.

BARDY: I was afraid I would lose you.

GRACE: Instead I had to lose you. And now it's all too late, isn't it.

BARDY: Is it?

GRACE: Yes, because you're not here.

BARDY: Then why did you come?

GRACE: To shout at my memories? I don't know.

BARDY stands before her. She looks down avoiding his eyes.

BARDY: Am I forgiven, Grace?

GRACE: If you were here, you would be. But you're not, so…

She looks up at him. BARDY sits and gently wraps his arms around her. GRACE shudders and then nestles into his embrace. They hold each other in silence for a moment. Then…

BARDY: I have to go now.

GRACE holds him more tightly.

GRACE: I know.

BARDY disengages himself but GRACE holds onto his hands.

BARDY: You can't go anywhere…unless you were somewhere to begin with.

She looks at him quizzically, still holding his hands.

And you can't let go of something you've never held…
You can do that now. It's all right.

GRACE looks down at his hands in hers, and gently releases them.

You don't really think it's all a muddle, do you?

GRACE: No, but I don't think it's a straight line, either. God isn't the answer to anything, he's the question. And faith doesn't sort out the mess, it simply allows you to join in.

BARDY smiles and nods agreement.

BARDY: How do I look? Do I look all right?

She straightens his tie and brushes his lapel with her hand.

GRACE: You look very handsome. I never imagined…

BARDY: You never 'imagined' what?

GRACE: That old age would so become you.

BARDY sets off towards the gap in the hedge leading to the stream. GRACE watches. He stops and turns.

BARDY: I'll see you later.

GRACE: When I'm ready, you can tell him from me – and not a minute before.

BARDY smiles…and is about to go when he hesitates…

BARDY: Give Jo my love.

GRACE: Yes I will. She misses you dreadfully.

BARDY: Yes I know. She was right to persuade that girl to come here.

GRACE: What girl?

BARDY: The vicar lady when she got cold feet. She's the best thing to have happened to this place since I arrived.

GRACE suddenly looks puzzled, realising what he has said. She is about to ask a question… But BARDY has gone.

JO enters.

JO: There you are! What are you doing here? I've only just got your message – we've been looking everywhere for you!

GRACE: Jo, I have to ask you something.

JO: Ask me on the way. We're late.

GRACE: No, now. It's important.

JO: Mum, Auntie Ruth is in the car and getting very agitated.

GRACE: Did Sarah ever tell you she had cold feet about coming here?

JO: What?

GRACE: Sarah. Did she?

JO: Yes. But it was a private discussion, and it's all in the past so don't go bringing it up now, for heaven's sake.

GRACE is looking distantly towards the exit that BARDY took.

How did you know, anyway? Did she tell you?… Mum?

GRACE looks joyfully distracted.

Look, we really do have to go you know.

SARAH reappears.

SARAH: Oh good. You found each other.

JO: Yes. Thank you. Sorry to have troubled you. We're just on our way.

SARAH: Oh it's no trouble, there's no hurry.

JO: Well, there is actually…

GRACE: No. There isn't. Five minutes won't hurt. Tell her about the stream, Sarah – I'm going to have a little poke about in here.

JO: Mum!

GRACE: You don't mind do you, Sarah?

SARAH: Not at all.

GRACE vanishes into the greenhouse.

JO: (*Pointing to her stomach.*) How's it going?

SARAH: Hanging on in there.

JO: Hang on long enough, and you'll be perfect casting for the nativity.

SARAH: Ha! Yes.

JO: So…it was a good decision, then?

SARAH: (*Resting her hands on her stomach.*) … Yes… Thank you.

Beat. JO sees GRACE rummaging around in the greenhouse.

JO: I gather she pops in from time to time?

SARAH: Yes. I see her face in the back pew.

JO: Not an intrusion?

SARAH: Not one bit. I'm glad she feels she can.

RUTH enters – a more strident figure now, and at speed.

RUTH: Is she here – that blasted sister of mine?

JO: She's in the greenhouse.

RUTH: She's what?!

SARAH: Hello, Ruth. How nice to see you.

RUTH: The greenhouse? What the blazes is she doing in there?… Hello Sarah. Sorry about this.

SARAH: She's having a little poke about.

RUTH: I'll give her a little poke about. Jo, we have to go.

JO: I know.

SARAH: Where are you off to? I thought you were back in Uganda.

RUTH: I have been. I was. I flew back last week – ahead of my son.

JO: He flies in today. That's where we're going.

SARAH: Oh, how exciting! You're meeting him for the first time?

JO: Yes, yes, but Mum's been a bit funny about it.

RUTH: We've all been treading on bloody egg shells.

JO: So…you know…best not to mention it.

SARAH: No. Of course.

RUTH: Oh, I'm not putting up with this…

RUTH goes over the greenhouse and bangs on the glass…

Grace!… Come out of there!

GRACE appears at the greenhouse door… Holding BARDY's old hat.

GRACE: Look what I've found.

RUTH: A hat. Marvellous. If you can find a bag and gloves to match, perhaps we can go?

JO: Good heavens. Dad's old gardening hat.

SARAH: Where on earth did you find it?

GRACE: On the hook on the wall. Where he always kept it.

SARAH: How odd. We cleaned the whole place out – I never noticed it.

GRACE looks at it affectionately.

RUTH: Grace, if we don't leave now we'll be late.

GRACE: Right. I'm ready. How do I look?

RUTH: Fine… No, hold on – you've got…

RUTH picks a small white feather off GRACE's shoulder.

It's all right it's a feather.

She lets it float to the ground.

You've been kissing angels again. Right, let's go.

GRACE sits on the bench, pulls a small mirror out of her bag and touches up her make-up.

GRACE: (*To SARAH.*) We're just off to meet Jo's brother, Sarah. Did they tell you?

SARAH: Yes. They did.

GRACE: Ruth's boy.

SARAH: Yes, of course.

GRACE: By my late husband.

SARAH: Yes. Well… Feel free to drop in any time, Mrs Thomas – the garden is always here for you.

GRACE: Thank you that's very kind, but I won't be bothering you again. Shall we go, Ruth?

RUTH: No, let's all sit here and knit a jumper.

GRACE: Oh, without speaking out of turn, Sarah, might I ask you a delicate question?

RUTH: No, Grace – you can't.

GRACE: Just quickly. I was wondering if the collar and the bump quite went together? I think you should wear either one or the other, don't you?

SARAH: Things have to move forward, Mrs Thomas.

GRACE: Do they.

SARAH: Yes.

GRACE: Forward.

SARAH: Yes.

GRACE: Oh dear. I feel it puts you at something of a disadvantage, that's all.

SARAH: Then I'm in good company.

GRACE: How so?

SARAH: Because when he came, he came as a child, born into poverty, he lived under tyranny and died in obscurity. He could hardly have been more disadvantaged.

GRACE smiles. She picks up BARDY's hat and is about to set off.

GRACE: Actually, he could.

SARAH: Could he? Really? how?

GRACE: He could have come as a woman.

Beat. All three women laugh as SARAH leads them out.

Blackout

The end.

WWW.OBERONBOOKS.COM

 Follow us on www.twitter.com/@oberonbooks
& www.facebook.com/OberonBooksLondon